THE HERO AND THE KING
AN EPIC THEME

W. T. H. JACKSON

THE HERO AND THE KING

 AN EPIC THEME

NEW YORK COLUMBIA UNIVERSITY PRESS 1982

Clothbound editions of Columbia University Press books are Smyth-sewn and printed on permanent and durable acid-free paper.

Library of Congress Cataloging in Publication Data

Jackson, W. T. H. (William Thomas Hobdell),
  1915-
  The hero and the king.

  Bibliography: p.
  1. Epic poetry, European—History and
criticism. 2. Heroes in literature. 3. Kings
and rulers in literature. I. Title.
PN1303.J3   809.1'3   81-12205
ISBN 0-231-05354-1   AACR2

Columbia University Press
New York   Guildford, Surrey

Copyright © 1982 Columbia University Press
All rights reserved

Printed in the United States of America

CONTENTS

PREFACE AND ACKNOWLEDGMENTS

This book is an attempt to show the importance of a single theme—the opposition between settled ruler and independent warrior—in the determining of epic structure. It will be noted that it is a study of *an* epic theme, not *the* epic theme. I am far from maintaining that the great Western European epics are important only as illustrations of this theme. Quite the contrary. Their greatness as individual works of art depends on quite different criteria. Nevertheless it seems to me that they can be better understood if it is recognized that a factor which was originally social, the decline or temporary weakness of a ruler who was faced with a younger man bent on establishing a reputation, played an important role in shaping the structure of what various peoples thought of as epic poetry.

Epics always have strong social overtones. They are always thought of as presenting some kind of model for behavior in a particular society, and the opposition between the settled and the intrusive, the old and the young, the retiring and the ambitious, became so much a concern of epic that it was virtually impossible to compose an epic poem without this structural element, even when the avowed purpose of the poem did not demand it.

The conflict does not appear in the same form in every work, and indeed it is the variations on the theme by individual poets, the use they make of it for their own purposes, which constitute its importance and which demonstrate how aware the authors were of its existence.

I have discussed in any detail only the major epics of Western literature and not all of those. Some I do not know well enough. Others, like Lucan's *Pharsalia*, are "artificial" epics with a sophisticated purpose far removed from that of traditional epic poetry. (It is perfectly possible, however, to show that even Lucan was well aware of the theme.) The fact of selection hardly invalidates the thesis, since the epics discussed spring from very different societies and are widely separated in time. No attempt has been made to include the medieval narrative poems usually called romances. These, too, have recognizable conventions, among them, in the Arthurian romances, a young hero and an old king. The conflict, however, when it occurs, is of a different kind and calls for a different approach.

The original texts have been quoted to support the more important statements; otherwise I have given line references. The translations are my own.

I would like to express my gratitude to the American Council of Learned Societies for its financial support of this (and several other) projects. My former student and friend Setsuko Ohara Haruta read the manuscript with her usual meticulous care. My research assistant Brian Spence went far beyond the call of duty in his bibliographical research on the epic and in his careful reading of the text. And the Columbia University Press has been as kind and understanding as it has always been in the twenty happy years of our relationship.

THE HERO AND THE KING
AN EPIC THEME

PART ONE

THE CONFLICT BETWEEN HERO AND KING

The study of epic poetry has always been bedeviled by religious, anthropological, and historical considerations. The fact that epics have been regarded by various generations of critics as "primitive," "naive," or "heroic" has led to their being used as evidence for the mores of certain societies and to the use of the "mores" thus established to prove something about the morality of the poems themselves. In reading many critics, particularly those of the nineteenth and early twentieth centuries, it is difficult to escape the conclusion that there was more interest in establishing the connection between ancient civilizations and Homer's Trojan War than in analyzing the *Iliad* as a poem, more interest in examining *Beowulf* and the *Nibelungenlied* as evidence for "Germanic" morality than as works of art.[1] Such an attitude is

1. The following works will give some idea of this critical attitude: Thomas Day Seymour, *Life in the Homeric Age* (New York: Macmillan, 1907; reprint; Biblo and Tannen, 1963); Denys Page, *History and the Homeric Iliad* (Berkeley: University of California Press, 1959); Gaston Paris, "*La Chanson de Roland* et les Nibelungen," *Revue germanique* (1963), 25: 292–302; M. Thausing, "Die Nibelungen: Ein Beitrag zur Frage über die Entstehungszeit des Liedes," *Germania* (1861), 6: 435–56; literature cited in Mary Thorp, *The Study of the Nibelungenlied* (Oxford: Clarendon Press, 1940), especially pp. 60ff., and in M. I. Finley, *The World of Odysseus* (rev ed.; New York: Viking Press, 1965).

dangerous, not least because it has led to the construction of certain pseudohistorical types of society or behavior which influence even those critics whose major concern is to interpret epics as poetry.

The themes of epic poetry are indeed closely tied to certain cultural features in society but not to particular features of a particular society. The nature of the armor and offensive weapons of Homer's warriors is of far less importance than the fact that in the *Iliad* and the *Odyssey* battles are decided by single combats, not by the use of masses of troops or tactical decisions of generals. This is true of all Western epic poetry but it is not necessarily true of the cultures with which they appear to be connected. No amount of research into the nature of Mycenaean or Germanic fighting will throw any light on epic combat as a poetical phenomenon, because the nature of combat in epics is determined by literary, not cultural considerations.

Any reader of epics knows that they rarely end in unqualified success for the principal character. *Beowulf* and the *Nibelungenlied* both end in stark tragedy. Not only do their heroes die, but the outlook for the civilizations they represent is grim indeed. Of Achilles and Aeneas it may be said that while their public life has been successful with the defeat of an enemy, their private lives are plunged in sadness and in the recognition of their lack of sympathy with other human beings. Charlemagne, already shattered by the loss of Roland, learns at the end of the poem that God demands yet more of him. Of the great Western epics only the *Odyssey* and the *Cid* end in a happiness which is apparently unalloyed, the former because it is a peacetime counterpart of the *Iliad*, a restitution of the society almost destroyed by war, the latter because it describes events so close to the time of composition that the pressures of epic form had little opportunity to exercise their effect. It is not too much to say that defeat and death are more likely to produce epic poetry than is victory. More important, perhaps, is the fact that epics spring from violent social disturbance, when patterns of civilization of long standing are being challenged or overturned—the troubled period after the collapse of the Cretan thalassocracy, the Germanic invasions of Western Europe, the clash between Christian and Moslem. Out of this turmoil comes one of the most important of all epic themes, the conflict of hero and king. The terms require some explanation. The word "hero" has been so abused in studies of epic poetry that it needs some reevaluation. In traditional criticism the word implies the possession of certain qualities—bravery, superhuman strength, success in battle, and contempt for wounds and death. It will be noted that these qualities have very little to do with the individual's attitude to society but are concerned exclusively with his personal behavior and primarily with the desire for fame which all heroes should display. The hero will almost always be of high birth, often of semidivine origin and hence highly influential. Yet these qualities are not in themselves remarkable in the warrior societies in which all epics are set. No man who did not possess these "heroic" qualities could ever hope to be noticed, and certainly not to achieve the kind of reputation which would survive his death and ensure everlasting fame. Heroes become interesting to us when their pattern of behavior departs from the purely "heroic," when Achilles shows pity to Priam, when Odysseus succeeds by intelligence rather than force, when Hagen pushes heroic qualities to their logical end of universal destruction. In themselves these "heroic" qualities are not remarkable enough to form the basis of a study of epic poetry. Bowra has remarked with justice that all heroic poetry is not epic poetry. One might go further and say that the term "heroic poetry" really says very little and is of no help whatsoever in studying epic poetry.

One quality often connected with heroes and heroic poetry has not been mentioned—the quality of loyalty. How important is it to the character of the hero in epics? No one would pretend that Achilles is loyal to Agamemnon or even the Greek cause, and Roland's loyalty to Charlemagne, like Siegfried's to Gunther, is seriously compromised. Only Beowulf shows the unhesitating devotion to his lord, his lord's family, and even to a temporary lord, Hrothgar, a quality which, we are told, is characteristic of the hero. Yet loyalty is not only an issue in all these poems but perhaps the most important issue. In all the major epics, except the *Odyssey*, there is tension because of the relation between a ruler and a major figure in the work. The tension may be discussed in terms of loyalty, and the formal situation in the epics is often such that loyalty to a ruler is demanded of a young and ambitious warrior. Yet the true situation is not so simple. The conflict between ruler and hero is often as much a conflict of values as of personalities and seems to be an essential theme of epic poetry. The reason is not far to seek. Epic themes spring from turmoil, and one of the characteristics of turmoil is the intrusion of the outsider into a settled, established culture, an outsider who often proves more powerful than the ruler to whose court he comes and who must be placated or, if necessary, suppressed, if he is not to dominate the court into which he intrudes.

It is highly probable that all epics reflect the conditions of turmoil we have mentioned but that does not mean that the composers of epics were always conscious of such historical and social conditions. The material they had received by oral transmission reflected those conditions, and the themes became so established that they were regarded as essential to the genre. We may posit a sequence like this: social turmoil (historical); selection of narrative elements as a result of certain incidents which impressed themselves most deeply on the consciousness of a relatively small social group; the rendering of these themes into poetry, in oral form and in numerous versions which would differ considerably in detail but would preserve the selected themes; the selection, accidental or deliberate, of one of these versions to be written down and, in all probability, to be revised many times before it appears in the versions we possess. In view of much that has been written about oral-formulaic poetry, it is not belaboring the obvious to stress that we have no record of the oral form of any of the great epics. The epics which we possess in manuscript form may be many times removed from their oral antecedents and may well have undergone substantial revision in their written form, no matter how many traces of oral-formulaic poetry may still be noted in them.

There can be little doubt that one of the most common characters in the "period of turmoil" is the exile from one's own culture. The breakdown of tribal organization and factionalism in social groups undoubtedly caused many young and ambitious men to leave their original milieu, either under compulsion, because they ran afoul of old rulers or new invaders, or because they believed their chances to be better in a new environment. About this kind of movement there can be little dispute, since Greek history and that of the Germanic peoples afford many examples of such movements—the colonies sent out from Greek towns, the Scandinavian expeditions to Russia, to Ireland, and to the Mediterranean. Both population pressure at home and the break-up of a tribe under foreign pressure produced the most characteristic of epic heroes, the exile.

There is no major epic in which the hero is not in some sense an exile. In the *Odyssey* the hero is kept away from Ithaca for more than half the work. Aeneas loses his homeland before the epic opens. Siegfried is seen at home only in the opening scenes of the *Nibelungenlied*. All his actions are performed either at Gunther's court or on his behalf. The fact that he is a foreigner is of supreme importance for the way in which he is treated and for the development of the epic. In the Norse version, of course, he is an exile in every sense, a man without a home or country. The Cid is formally exiled by his king before the poem begins, and it is the desire for a reversal of that sentence and permission to return to court which motivates all his actions. Waltharius, in the Latin poem of the same title, is a hostage at the court of Attila, and his exploits are those of a stranger in a strange land, since he leaves that court only to fall foul of the Burgundian King Gunther as he makes his way home. Beowulf is never technically an exile, since he leaves the kingdom of Hygelac voluntarily and returns to it after the killing of Grendel's mother but again, before he becomes king, all the exploits mentioned in the poem are carried out away from his own country and among strangers. The few companions he takes with him have no part in his adventures.

In some of the epics the hero does not *appear* to be an exile in any sense. Achilles is fighting with fellow Greeks against Troy. All are far from home, a fact frequently stressed in the *Iliad*, but they are one body under an elected commander-in-chief. There is evidence, however, that Achilles is an outsider. He comes from a remote region of the Greek-speaking world and he is not a king in the Homeric sense that he rules over land. He has been recruited because he is the greatest fighting man available and because Troy cannot be taken without him. His reason for being with the Greek host is purely a desire for glory, for the enduring fame which has been promised him in lieu of a long uneventful life. In this respect he conforms to the "heroic" pattern exactly, for he chooses fame over life. It may be remarked that his shade, in the *Odyssey*, is of a very different opinion. This feeling of being an outsider is of great significance in the development of the *Iliad* and for its total ethic, for it is a clear illustration of the feeling by one of the characters in an epic of the difference between a hero and a king.

The status of Roland in the *Chanson de Roland* is even more difficult to reconcile with that of an exile. He is a close associate of Charlemagne and is his nephew,[2] and there is no evidence that he has come from another culture or court. He is, of course, fighting on foreign soil, but so are all the emperor's forces. He is not even like Guillaume d'Orange, forced to fight the Saracens for territory "granted" to him by his king. What characteristics, then, does he share with the exile? First, his great battle has to be fought as an individual, separated from his king and the main body of his forces, for although he has the rear guard with him, his conduct of the operation is entirely his own, and his desire for fame and reluctance to seek help decide his own fate and that

2. There were stories that Roland was Charlemagne's son by an incestuous union. See the literature cited by Gerard J. Brault, *The Song of Roland*, vol. 1, Introduction and Commentary (University Park: Pennsylvania State University Press, 1978), pp. 375 and 397.

of his companions. Much more important, however, is the characteristic which he shares with all the exiles we have mentioned, a characteristic which determines the very nature of epic poetry, his opposition to Charlemagne and hence to the ruling establishment. The exile inevitably finds himself in conflict with the ruling establishment. He is from a different culture, younger than the ruler, and ambitious to establish himself in his new environment. It is this conflict, which originates in historical circumstances, that provides the motivation of all Western epics, even though the hero may not be in an exact sense an exile. Let us examine them from this point of view.

The *Iliad* begins with exposition of this conflict, and its roots are of some importance. Agamemnon is called upon to give up Chryseis, the daughter of the Trojan priest of Apollo. She has been assigned to him as booty and, by the standards of the time, he is entitled to her. He has to give her up because Chryses, priest of Apollo, has begged the god to help him and Apollo is raining destruction on the Greek army.[3]

«κλῦθί μευ, ἀργυρότοξ, ὃς Χρύσην ἀμφιβέβηκας
Κίλλαν τε ζαθέην Τενέδοιό τε ἶφι ἀνάσσεις,
Σμινθεῦ, εἴ ποτέ τοι χαρίεντ᾽ ἐπὶ νηὸν ἔρεψα,
ἢ εἰ δή ποτέ τοι κατὰ πίονα μηρί᾽ ἔκηα
ταύρων ἠδ᾽ αἰγῶν, τόδε μοι κρήηνον ἐέλδωρ·
τείσειαν Δαναοὶ ἐμὰ δάκρυα σοῖσι βέλεσσιν.»   I, 37-42

(Hear me, you of the silver bow who bestride Chrysa and holy Cilla and mightily rule over the islands of Tenedos. Smintheus, if ever I set up a temple that rejoiced your heart or if ever I burned fat thighs of bulls or goats for you, grant this my desire: Let your shafts make the Danaeans pay for my tears.)

The significant point about this incident is that it is in his capacity as leader that Agamemnon must give up his prize. There is much

---

3. *Homeri opera*, Thomas W. Allen, ed. Vols. 1 and 2: *Iliad* (3d ed.; Oxford: Clarendon Press, 1920).

evidence in the Greek culture of the preclassical period, as in many others, that the king must sacrifice himself for his people, even if this involves his death.[4] Agamemnon is the supreme leader of the Greeks and in return for this honor he must accept the responsibilities. In this case the loss is slight—a captive woman. Yet Agamemnon refuses to behave as a king should. He regards his loss as an insult rather than the fulfillment of a responsibility, and his first thought is to ensure that he will not suffer any personal loss of property or prestige. To effect this he orders Achilles to give up his legitimate prize of war, Briseis.

ἔχθιστος δέ μοί ἐσσι διοτρεφέων βασιλήων·
αἰεὶ γάρ τοι ἔρις τε φίλη πόλεμοί τε μάχαι τε·
εἰ μάλα καρτερός ἐσσι, θεός που σοὶ τό γ᾽ ἔδωκεν·
οἴκαδ᾽ ἰὼν σὺν νηυσί τε σῆς καὶ σοῖς ἑτάροισι
Μυρμιδόνεσσιν ἄνασσε, σέθεν δ᾽ ἐγὼ οὐκ ἀλεγίζω,
οὐδ᾽ ὄθομαι κοτέοντος· ἀπειλήσω δέ τοι ὧδε·
ὡς ἔμ᾽ ἀφαιρεῖται Χρυσηΐδα Φοῖβος Ἀπόλλων,
τὴν μὲν ἐγὼ σὺν νηΐ τ᾽ ἐμῇ καὶ ἐμοῖς ἑτάροισι
πέμψω, ἐγὼ δέ κ᾽ ἄγω Βρισηΐδα καλλιπάρῃον
αὐτὸς ἰὼν κλισίηνδε, τὸ σὸν γέρας, ὄφρ᾽ ἐΰ εἰδῇς
ὅσσον φέρτερός εἰμι σέθεν, στυγέῃ δὲ καὶ ἄλλος
ἶσον ἐμοὶ φάσθαι καὶ ὁμοιωθήμεναι ἄντην.»   I, 176-87

(Of all the kings nurtured by Zeus, you were always the most hostile to me, for strife was ever dear to you, and war, and fighting. If you are indeed stronger, it was a god who made you the gift. Go home with your ships and your comrades and rule over your Myrmidons, for I care nothing for you nor do I heed you in your anger. But be warned. Since Phoebus Apollo has taken Chryseis away from me, I shall send her in my ship with my companions, and I myself will go to your hut and take Briseis of the fair face, your prize, so that you may really know how much greater I am than you and so that any other man may fear to proclaim himself my equal and equate himself with me face to face.)

4. For examples of the sacrificial king, see James G. Frazer, *The Golden Bough: A Study in Magic and Religion* (3d ed.; New York: Macmillan, 1935) and Joseph Campbell, *The Hero with a Thousand Faces* (New York: Pantheon, 1949).

Agamemnon's deed precipitates all the action in the *Iliad*, and its reason must therefore be determined. Why does he choose to humiliate Achilles and not some less important warrior whose loss would be of no significance to the Greek forces? Even a powerful but reasonable person such as Odysseus would have been a better choice. Agamemnon can have had only one motivation for such an action, an unthinking determination to prove that, even if he had to yield to the god, he could command absolute obedience from even the most powerful and most essential warrior in his command. In doing so he betrayed his inability to act as a king and even to think as a king. He thinks in terms of personal power.

Achilles has no such responsibilities. He is needed by the Greeks if they wish to capture Troy but he is not called upon to behave as king. He is not the supreme commander nor does he have any royal religious functions. He does know, however, that he is doomed to die before Troy and in that respect he is being called upon to sacrifice himself as a king might do.

μήτηρ γάρ τέ μέ φησι θεὰ Θέτις ἀργυρόπεζα
διχθαδίας κῆρας φερέμεν θανάτοιο τέλοσδε.
εἰ μέν κ᾽ αὖθι μένων Τρώων πόλιν ἀμφιμάχωμαι,
ὤλετο μέν μοι νόστος, ἀτὰρ κλέος ἄφθιτον ἔσται·
εἰ δέ κεν οἴκαδ᾽ ἵκωμι φίλην ἐς πατρίδα γαῖαν,
ὤλετό μοι κλέος ἐσθλόν, ἐπὶ δηρὸν δέ μοι αἰὼν
ἔσσεται, οὐδέ κέ μ᾽ ὦκα τέλος θανάτοιο κιχείη.   IX, 410-16

(For my mother, the goddess Thetis of the silver feet, tells me that there are two kinds of fate which lead me toward my end in death. If I stay here and go on besieging the city of Troy, my return home is gone and my fame will live forever; but if I go home to the dear land of my fathers, gone is my shining glory, but my life will long continue nor will death's end come to me till late.)

But Achilles has none of the privileges which should accompany such a sacrifice. He feels, rightly, that it is he who is being called upon to play the role of king, while Agamemnon exploits his role for personal ends. Neither Achilles nor Agamemnon "feels" anything, of course. The author of the *Iliad* regards the conflict between king and outsider-hero as an essential feature of epic poetry and he makes it the central feature of the poem. The *Iliad* is not a poem about the siege of Troy but about the conflict between two different points of view. Agamemnon regards himself as supreme in every sense, even to the extent that he may take actions that will prejudice the success of the very expedition of which he was appointed supreme commander. He thus reverses the role to which he was appointed and, to the extent that he has failed his office, Achilles is justified in his actions. By withdrawing the fighting services which should be the sole contribution required of him, he makes clear the deficiencies of Agamemnon as a ruler. Zeus, too, recognizes these deficiencies, for he agrees with Thetis' plea that the Greeks should recognize the effect of Achilles' absence by being defeated by the Trojans.

There is, however, another aspect of the quarrel. Selfish or not, Agamemnon is the supreme king, as Nestor takes care to point out to Achilles, and if his authority is challenged, the fabric of the military organization he commands is in danger.

μήτε σύ, Πηλείδη, ἔθελ᾽ ἐριζέμεναι βασιλῆϊ
ἀντιβίην, ἐπεὶ οὔ ποθ᾽ ὁμοίης ἔμμορε τιμῆς
σκηπτοῦχος βασιλεύς, ᾧ τε Ζεὺς κῦδος ἔδωκεν.
εἰ δὲ σὺ καρτερός ἐσσι, θεὰ δέ σε γείνατο μήτηρ,
ἀλλ᾽ ὅ γε φέρτερός ἐστιν, ἐπεὶ πλεόνεσσιν ἀνάσσει. I, 277-81

(And you, son of Peleus, do not choose to oppose face to face a king in strife, for a scepter-bearing king is allotted honor beyond the norm. To him Zeus has given glory. Even though you may be stronger and a goddess bore you, yet he is the greater, since he rules over more men.)

Achilles' defiance thus has very serious implications. If one warrior can challenge authority, others can do so too, and the near-chaos at the council shows how conscious Homer was of the problem. The fact that Odysseus has to deal so harshly with Thersites shows what could happen (II, 212 ff.). The more sober

Greeks, particularly Odysseus, are deeply concerned at the possible results. The rights of Achilles and Agamemnon as individuals are as nothing compared with the cause for which they have come to Troy. A deep-seated principle of all epic poetry is involved here, that public matters are more important than private, and that the great men of the epic must subordinate their private desire to their public duty. Agamemnon fails this test until it is brought home to him by the defeat of his army. Does Achilles fail it too?

Achilles' reaction to Agamemnon's demand is provoked by the fact that he is not receiving recognition as the indispensable champion of the Greeks. The fame for which he had agreed to barter a long life is being denied him. The Greek cause is nothing to him, as he soon proves by asking for its representatives to be defeated and by standing idly by when the defeats occur. He is impervious to pleas by senior leaders and reenters the fight entirely on personal grounds, when Patroclus is killed by Hector. The culminating battle before the walls of Troy is an act of revenge by Achilles, as the treatment of the body of Hector proves. The fact that, in killing Hector, Achilles removes Troy's greatest warrior is incidental. In fact it does not bring Troy any nearer to defeat, as the Troy stories not in the *Iliad* show.[5] Achilles is a greater human being after the interview with Priam, but his reconciliation with Agamemnon seems superficial. Each blames the gods and fate.

> Ἕκτορι μὲν καὶ Τρωσὶ τὸ κέρδιον· αὐτὰρ᾽ Ἀχαιοὺς
> δηρὸν ἐμῆς καὶ σῆς ἔριδος μνήσεσθαι ὀΐω.
> ἀλλὰ τὰ μὲν προτετύχθαι ἐάσομεν ἀχνύμενοί περ,
> θυμὸν ἐνὶ στήθεσσι φίλον δαμάσαντες ἀνάγκῃ·
> νῦν δ᾽ ἤτοι μὲν ἐγὼ παύω χόλον, οὐδέ τί με χρὴ
> ἀσκελέως αἰεὶ μενεαινέμεν·   XIX, 63-68

5. Later works speak of treason within Troy, led by Aeneas and Antenor. See *Anonymi Historia Troyana Daretis Frigii, Untersuchungen und kritische Ausgabe* von Jürgen Stohlmann (Ratingen: Henn 1968) and Dictys Cretensis, *Ephemeridos belli Troiani libri*, Werner Eisenhut, ed. (2d ed.; Leipzig: Teubner, 1973).

(It was a gain for Hector and the Trojans. But I think the Achaeans will long remember the strife between you and me. Let the past be past, sad though we may be, and let us submit the dear hearts in our breasts to necessity. I at least now put by my anger, for it is not right that I should stay obstinately wrathful for ever.)

ἐγὼ δ᾽ οὐκ αἴτιός εἰμι,
ἀλλὰ Ζεὺς καὶ Μοῖρα καὶ ἠεροφοῖτις Ἐρινύς,
οἵ τέ μοι εἰν ἀγορῇ φρεσὶν ἔμβαλον ἄγριον ἄτην,
ἤματι τῷ ὅτ᾽ Ἀχιλλῆος γέρας αὐτὸς ἀπηύρων.   XIX, 86-89

(I am not the cause but Zeus and Fate and the Fury who walks in darkness, who put bitter hatred in my heart in the assembly on the day when I myself took his prize from Achilles.)

In this poem, Homer is making the earliest presentation in European literature of the conflict between the established king and the intruder-hero. It is the business of the king to maintain his dominion—in the *Iliad*, the force entrusted to him—at all costs. Not for nothing is he the shepherd of the people. If the only way to do this is to sacrifice his property or his life, he must do so. The hero, on the other hand, is under no such restraint. Whatever his social rank, even if he is the son of a king, he has no responsibility for the society into which he intrudes. He has only one object, the establishing of his own reputation. His responsibility extends at most to his immediate followers. He can do this in many ways—by conquering an enemy, by persuading the king to accept him as an indispensable adjunct to his court, by calling on a minstrel to sing his fame. The hero's objectives are thus personal, so far as his own life is concerned. He need not work for the good of society, and the conflict in the epic frequently occurs because the intruder-hero is concerned with his own fame even when the pursuit of fame does not contribute to the well-being of society. His conduct may be and often is detrimental to the society in which he moves and may be disturbing to the form of that society and the power and position of its leader.

Achilles sees his role as a warrior called in to help the Greeks, even though he has no personal or political stake in their victory. His only reason for participating is the acquisition of fame and honor. Agamemnon, on the other hand, has an obligation which springs from his position. All his actions should be determined by public policy, not personal convenience. His conduct toward Achilles is thus indefensible. He alienates the greatest of his warriors on purely personal grounds and comes close to destroying the cause he represents. He is the first in a long line of epic kings who are unable to carry out their functions. He is too weak to force Achilles to his viewpoint, too obstinate to yield gracefully and win the hero back.

The poem thus raises the essential question: what should be the relation between the preserver of stability and the dynamic intruder? Agamemnon fails because he has no conception of the true nature of kingship. He is still acting as a small regional king. Achilles too is wrong because he overstresses the respect due to his services and puts it above the common good. Homer, however, raises Achilles above the mere intruder by the conduct he ascribes to him at the end of the poem. Although he had behaved like a savage to obtain his revenge for the death of Patroclus, he shows true nobility in his conduct to Priam (xxiv, 366 ff.). It is Achilles' conduct, not Agamemnon's, which sets a standard of kingly behavior and shows what should happen in a stable society.

The relationship between Agamemnon and Achilles should be contrasted with that between Priam and Hector. Although he is the greatest Trojan warrior, Hector never comes into conflict with Priam. He carries out the policy of the king of Troy and is quite prepared to sacrifice his own well-being in the interest of that policy. The often-cited farewell scene between Hector, Andromache, and Astyanax has the function of demonstrating that Hector will not allow his family affections to interfere with his social duties. His attitude is that of the hero in the best sense, not the intruder-warrior. Homer emphasizes his love for Andromache in a fashion which would be inconceivable in describing the relationship between Agamemnon and Chryseis or Achilles and Briseis, but that love is not significant in determining what his action should be. In the same way Priam puts aside his own feelings in the interest of Troy. Priam's city represents a stable society unaffected by the intruder-hero and, in the *Iliad*, unaffected by dissension within.

The Greeks are in perpetual crisis because their king cannot control the intruder-warrior without whose help they cannot be successful. Achilles is never reconciled with Agamemnon except in the formal sense of accepting his oath that he had never taken Briseis into his bed. Later epics and even the prose Troy stories of Dares and Dictys always emphasize the disagreement between Achilles and the Greek leaders, even when the cause of it is totally different. It is not too much to say that the essential element of the *Iliad* is the conflict between Agamemnon, the inefficient representative of the Greek leadership and the self-centered, fame-seeking Achilles. The intruder-warrior comes very near to wrecking the Greek cause, and when he changes his mind, the reason is not that cause but his personal attachment to Patroclus. An obsession with personal fame is an immense danger to the social fabric.

The *Iliad* demonstrates clearly enough the features of the conflict between overlord and hero, between established and intrusive power. But because all the Greeks are exiles in the sense that they are fighting far from their homelands against a settled and firmly entrenched power, some features of the conflict between king and hero are not clearly brought out and it may be well to outline at this point what can be regarded as standard features of this conflict as it appears in many though not all the epics to be discussed.

The hero arrives at a court, usually one of which he has at least heard, accompanied by a band of followers. This band is rarely large enough to be called an army and never strong enough to overwhelm the settled community by sheer force. Some member of the court, or a watchman, brings news of the arrival, and the newcomers are asked to identify themselves. In doing so the intruder-hero gives some details of his ancestry and prowess, or a member of the court does so because the hero's fame has preceded him. The most important fact to be determined is the purpose of the visit, and in this regard there is a good deal of difference between the epics. Sometimes there is a direct challenge to the established power, but such an action is rare. More frequently the intruder takes up a task for the ruler and in doing so makes himself indispensable. There is a presumption that he may take over the land in which he has arrived or become so strong that he dictates the way it shall be ruled. Resentment is often aroused among those members of the court who were used to exercising that power and the struggle which develops may end in the death of the intruder or of the original members of the court. In every instance, whatever the outcome of the conflict, the political and social features of the court are radically changed.

The pattern of the conflict between settled king and intruder-hero is thus essentially a study of transfer of power or, in other terms, of the problem of kingship. In none of the major classical and medieval epics are we presented with a "normal" king, that is, with a king at the peak of his physical prowess, fully in control of his kingdom, with no problems, actual or potential, in his relations with his subjects or within himself. The sovereign may be powerful, with a slight flaw, or be guilty of a temporary weakness or aberration, or he may be weak and totally unworthy of his office. The intruder may be (but rarely is) a crude braggart, distinguished only by his physical strength and verbal pugnacity, but more often he is a powerful warrior of such caliber as to be worthy of kingship. The conflict between ruler and intruder-hero can often be seen, therefore, in terms of one generation's replacing another or of the need to provide adequate succession. At the center of the conflict is the fear which haunted all warrior societies, that of the chaos which would inevitably ensue if the ruler were to be too weak to carry out his office adequately or if an outsider were to take over who was determined to force alien ideas on their societies. All epics concern themselves directly with the problem of kingship, and we shall see how they use the details of the theme of the conflict between settled ruler and intruder-hero to present what, to each epic author, were the most important features of that problem.

The *Aeneid* was written with a clear purpose in mind, to provide respectability for Rome and particularly for the family and policies of Augustus. It might, therefore, be expected that it would avoid the conflict we have observed in the *Iliad*. Vergil uses material from the *Iliad* and *Odyssey* and from numerous other sources, most of which are known to us only from the scholiasts and mention by other authors. Since he is so eclectic, it is clear that he could have eliminated any elements of the intruder-warriors in his efforts to build up the character of his "new hero." Yet the intruder-warrior is very much in evidence.

We should note that for more than half of the poem Aeneas is the exile-intruder. We see him first in the classic situation, storm driven on to a foreign (and, to Vergil's audience, a hostile) shore (I, 157 ff.). He is received as a destitute individual, lacking in military power. The account he gives of his earlier career emphasizes this destitution. He had been driven from Troy, he had lost his wife, he had suffered all the miseries of Odysseus and more, he had lost the father for whom he had sacrificed his wife. The only thing that distinguished him from a thousand others was his sense of destiny and the many ambiguous signs from the gods that he had a new home and a new land to rule.

Yet within a few months this intruder is virtually king of Carthage, a rich town, settled and powerful. He has achieved this not by force of arms but by his sexual appeal to Queen Dido. We are told of an elaborate plot by Juno to continue her avenging ways against Troy by involving Aeneas with Dido against Jupiter's wishes, and of Venus' acquiescence in the plot (IV, 90 ff.). But Vergil provides enough motivation without any divine machinery. Dido is lonely in her self-imposed chastity, and Aeneas is a handsome, kingly stranger. She accepts him in her loneliness, he yields in his weariness:

> Si non pertaesum thalami taedaeque fuisset,
> Huic una forsan potui succumbere culpae. (IV, 18 f.)[6]

> (If I had not been totally weary of the marriage bed and the marriage flame, I might possibly have succumbed to temptation this once.)

On a human level they are two persons who desperately need consolation, and Vergil so portrays them. As characters in an epic, however, they should behave differently. Dido's duty as a queen is the preservation of the kingdom she has founded and, until the arrival of Aeneas, she had fulfilled this task admirably. Carthage was a hive of activity. Her infatuation with Aeneas changes the situation completely. Work changes to pleasure. When she is not hunting, she is day-dreaming, and the poet employs all the images of civilized idleness. It is no wonder that Fama is able to obtain a hearing and that the fame Dido has gained changes to infamy.

> Nunc media Aenean secum per moenia ducit,
> Sidoniasque ostentat opes, urbemque paratam;
> Incipit effari, mediaque in voce resistit:
> Nunc eadem, labente die, convivia quaerit,
> Iliacos iterum demens audire labores
> Exposcit, pendetque iterum narrantis ab ore. (IV, 74–79)

> (Sometimes she takes Aeneas with her through the fortifications, keeps pointing out the wealth of Sidon and the city's preparations; she starts to say something and breaks off halfway. Sometimes, as daylight fails, she tries to recreate that banquet scene and in her madness begs to hear again the sufferings of the Trojans and again she hangs upon Aeneas' lips as he tells his story.)

6. Quotations from R. A. B. Mynors, ed., *P. Vergilii Maronis opera* (Oxford: Clarendon Press, 1969).

Her personal preoccupation brings all public works to a halt, and Vergil uses striking imagery to express this effect of private emotion on the welfare of the state:

> Non coeptae adsurgunt turres; non arma iuventus
> exercet portusue aut propugnacula bello
> tuta parant: pendent opera interrupta minaeque
> murorum ingentes aequataque machina caelo. (IV, 86–89)

> (The towers she had begun stopped rising, the young people no longer practice with their weapons nor do they equip the ports or secure outworks for war; the works are broken off and hang fire, the mighty looming walls and the engine that touches the sky.)

Vergil uses the figure of Iarbas to call the attention of the reader to Dido's deficiencies (IV, 198 ff.). His is the voice of jealousy, but his prayer to Jupiter nevertheless points out her weakness as a queen, the fact that she has accepted a stranger as master— "*dominum* Aenean in regna recepit"—and a degenerate master at that. Dido had already tricked Iarbas out of land for the city when she was herself an exile, and he now sees the pattern of alien dominance repeated. Iarbas' resentment is justified. Penetration of the royal court by an exile is one of the dominant features of epic poetry, and his anger was to find its echo later in Hagen's address to the dying Siegfried. Aeneas is ordered to leave by Jupiter because his destiny lies elsewhere (IV, 223 ff.), and Dido perishes not only because of despair at losing Aeneas but because she genuinely believes that she is being punished for her breaking of the vow she had made when her husband Sychaeus died:

> "non licuit thalami expertem sine crimine uitam
> degere more ferae, talis nec tangere curas;
> non servata fides cineri promissa Sychaeo." (IV, 550–552)

> (I was not allowed to spend my life like a wild animal, without any marriage and without sin, untouched by any of these

cares. I did not keep the promise I made to the ashes of Sychaeus.)[7]

Essentially, she and Aeneas are guilty of the same fault. Each is prepared to give up kingship for sexual indulgence. Jupiter is concerned for Aeneas and not for Dido but, in the context, Dido is more guilty. She is sacrificing a kingdom for which she is already responsible, whereas Aeneas is merely postponing his destiny. He is still the exile without royal responsibility, whatever his future may be. His behavior, however heinous from the point of view of personal relations, is consistent with his role as intruder-hero, and he requires divine admonition to remind him of a greater destiny.

When Aeneas arrives in Italy, his role changes. The long preview of Rome's history makes his destiny certain. Nevertheless it is as an intruder-hero that he appears on the Latin scene, and Vergil follows a very common pattern in describing his arrival: a swarm of bees settles on a laurel sacred to Apollo and this is interpreted as foretelling the arrival of strangers—"'externum cernimus,' inquit /'adventare virum'" (VII, 68 f.). The first word of the prophecy is "stranger," and consultation with the sacred grove of Albumea makes clear to King Latinus that his daughter must marry this stranger and not the Latin Turnus to whom she had been promised. The seeds of discord have been sown and the political marriage is in sharp contrast to the relationship with Dido.

Aeneas follows a strict pattern in his approach to Latinus. He selects a group of ambassadors and these are able to see the military training of the Latin youth as they approach the court (VII, 165 ff.). Vergil, as so often, has modified the more primitive image, seen in the Beowulf and Siegfried stories, of the armed warriors who throng the ruler's court and are often a threat to

7. The translation reflects the generally accepted interpretation of the passage, but it seems to me that it could also mean "It was not right that I should spend my life like an animal, without a real marriage and still be without sin and unaffected by wretchedness such as this."

the new arrivals. The king is seen in all the splendor of a well-established court—and it is made clear that he is an old man, long past the age of personal combat. His is a settled, peaceful regime. There is one important departure from convention: he has no need to ask who the strangers are. He does ask what has brought them to his shores—storms at sea or a wrong course. These are the usual questions, for the appearance of strangers, particularly a large and well-armed band of strangers, was always a threat. The next step would be to enquire the ancestry and relationships of the stranger, but here Latinus is able to supply information and answer the question which has puzzled Aeneas and his band: how are they seeking the land of their ancestors?

> atque equidem memini (fama est obscurior annis)
> Auruncos ita ferre senes, his ortus ut agris
> Dardanus Idaeas Phrygiae penetrarit ad urbes. . . . (VII, 205–207)

Vergil has neatly used the epic convention of establishing the antecedents of the intruder-hero to justify the connection between Rome and Troy and incidentally to show that the Latins were the older race. Both Aeneas and Latinus are dignified by the disclosure.

The messenger sent by Aeneas replies in due form. He compliments Latinus by a reference to his divine ancestry, says that his company was not storm driven but has come purposely to Latium (VII, 212 ff.). The storm which has brought them here is of a different nature—the tempest which swept away Troy. Further, the gods themselves are responsible for Aeneas' directing his course to Latium. He promises that Latinus will not regret granting them a little land ("sedem exiguam") on which to settle and he offers Latinus very significant gifts—the libation bowl of Anchises and the rod, scepter, tiara, and vestments of Priam (VII, 247 f.). These kingly emblems clearly indicate a *translatio imperii*, not only of regal but of sacerdotal power from Troy back to Italy. Neither the messenger nor Aeneas knows of the possibility that

Lavinia will be betrothed to "the stranger," but if she is, their children will thus inherit the sacerdotal kingship both of Latium and Troy.

Vergil's intention is clear. He uses the standard epic form for the approach of the exiled hero to the established king but he prepares the reader for the outcome, by the insertion of divine omens and prophecies. The intruder-hero will be well received, and there will be no conflict with the king himself. On the contrary, the hero will aid the king, as he does in *Beowulf, Waltharius*, and other epics. Nevertheless the intruder-hero does not bring peace. His arrival shatters the harmonious arrangements which had been made for the succession. Latinus is described as elderly and he has no son. By marrying his daughter to a powerful local chieftain, peaceful succession can be secured. Like Hrothgar and Gunther, Louis the Pious and Attila (in some epics), Latinus lacks the power to control his own destiny or even his own people. Vergil, for obvious reasons, does not show him as criminally ineffective, as Gunther is in the *Nibelungenlied*, but he is a king at the mercy of forces beyond his control. Vergil stresses the supernatural powers which bring about war and chaos—Alecto stirred up by Juno—but even if we take such interference at the most literal level, the destruction wrought as a result of that interference is due to one cause and one only—the arrival of Aeneas and the Trojans. Juno did not hate Latins.

The actions of Turnus are, in fact, inescapable in the epic tradition. Whenever the intruder-hero does not oppose a strong king and attempt to oust him, he will fall foul of a principal warrior or advisor of a weak king, with devastating results for the kingdom. The speech of Alecto to Turnus makes clear all the resentments which a native-born nobleman would feel and which always occur in this epic situation.

"Turne, tot incassum fusos patiere labores,
et tu Dardaniis transcribi sceptra colonis?
rex tibi coniugium et quaesitas sanguine dotes
abnegat, externusque in regnum quaeritur heres.

i nunc, ingratis offer te, inrise, periclis;
Tyrrhenas, i, sterne acies, tege pace Latinos.
....
                                                        rex ipse Latinus,
ni dare coniugium et dicto parere fatetur,
sentiat et tandem Turnum experiatur in armis." (VII, 421–434)

(Turnus, are you going to allow all your hard work to go for
nothing and your royal rights to be handed over to Trojan
farmers? The king is denying you the marriage and the dowry
you pursued in blood. It is an heir from abroad who is now
sought after for the kingship. So go along, you poor fool, and
take on risks which bring you no profit; shatter the ranks of
the Tyrrhenians and bring peace to the Latins. . . . Let King
Latinus himself feel this and let him experience in person
what Turnus is really like in battle—unless he states that he
will keep his word and agree to the marriage.)

The thoughts of Turnus—if we assume that Alecto is reflecting
those thoughts in her appeal—revolve around certain features:
the ingratitude of the Latin leadership, the loss of the chance of
supreme power, and the fact that he is being supplanted by a
foreigner. "Tu" is juxtaposed to "Dardaniis," "sceptra" with
"colonis," "externus" stands between "abnegat" and "regnum." Turnus sees force as his only resort and he determines to
bring peace through war and to let King Latinus discover Turnus'
true power as a warrior by defeating him. The reaction is typical
of the native threatened by the intruder-hero, not only in its resentment of the promotion of a foreigner to the king's favor but
in its determination to use violence to prove superiority and to
gain revenge. Alecto's speech ends with a succession of violent
images, violently expressed. The more reasonable attitude of
Turnus (lines 435–44) is soon swept away in a tumult of angry
feelings.

For the remainder of the poem Vergil presents Turnus almost
entirely in terms of violent action and almost irrational behavior
(e.g., IX, 18 ff.). He moves in the midst of a war which is internecine, for the number of Trojans involved is small. The war is

fought between Latins, Rutulians, Volscians, and Etruscans, as well as other major Italian peoples. Nisus and Euryalus (IX, 176 ff.) are the only Trojans of note to figure in incidents which compare in pathos with the deaths of their young ally Pallas (X, 474 ff.), or of Lausus (X, 811 ff.) and Camilla (XI, 794 ff.), both of whom are opponents of Aeneas and the invaders. Vergil wished, of course, to stress the "Italian" aspects of the war, the fact that it prefigured in myth the historical struggle of Latium for the hegemony of Italy. Yet there is no denying that the coming of Aeneas has destroyed the peace of Italy and brought with it chaos and the slaughter of many of the finest of the Italian youth, a slaughter which the weak kings Latinus and Evander are powerless to prevent. Peace comes only with the defeat of the jealous native, Turnus, by the intruder-hero, Aeneas.

Throughout the *Aeneid*, Vergil shows Aeneas as an exile intruder-hero. At Carthage he can fill this role in a fashion which conforms to the normal epic pattern, except that he destroys the incumbent ruler not by arms or physical force but by sexual attraction. His second intrusion is into Italy, where he is destined to rule, and there Vergil had a much harder problem. He could not portray Aeneas in violent opposition to the ruling King Latinus, since it was part of his purpose to stress the legitimacy of Roman rule. To present Aeneas as a pirate and ravisher would have destroyed the illusion. Furthermore, Aeneas must be presented in the later books as an increasingly kingly figure. The solution is the normal alternative to the intruder-hero who defeats and displaces the ruler or who simply brings discord and violence to a normal peaceful realm, namely to present Aeneas as a person innocent of disruption but to produce that disruption through the impotence of a noble, well-meaning, but aging king and the jealousy of a native warrior whose privileged position and, in this poem, right of succession, are being challenged by the intruder-hero.

By choosing this solution, Vergil is able to free Aeneas from personal blame for the destruction caused by his arrival, but it cannot be denied that in using it he does little to dispel the tension which is one of the great weaknesses of his epic: what is Aeneas? We are told that he is the ancestor of Rome but we never see him as a ruler. He is an exile driven from place to place with little control over his own destiny and consequently he never behaves like a true intruder-hero, whose main characteristics are independence of action and capacity for disruption. Aeneas is at home neither as hero nor as king, and we are often as uncomfortable with his role as he himself appears to be.

The medieval epics written in Latin and strongly influenced by Vergil show the pattern of hero opposed to king. The *Excidium Troiae* of Joseph Iscanus presents the portrait of Achilles which is standard in medieval works, based on the late classical romanticized prose accounts ascribed to Dares and Dictys.[8] His opposition to the Greek leaders, not only to Agamemnon, is not due to his being deprived of his prize but because of a more fundamental disagreement. He falls in love with Polyxena, a daughter of Priam, and wishes to arrange a peace with the Trojans so that he can marry her. He thus demands a total reversal of Greek policy and, in effect, insists that his individual wishes be set ahead of the interests for which the army was assembled, in other words, that private needs be preferred to public. It is small wonder that this version appealed to writers of romance, whose object was to stress the role of the individual and to show society as a context within which and sometimes in opposition to which the hero can demonstrate his innate characteristics. It would be unthinkable in a true epic that love for a woman could be the cause of such a fundamental action on the part of the intruder-hero. Yet the sentimentalizing of the material does not remove the essential theme of the breach between the established ruler and the disruptive hero.

The *Waltharius manu fortis* has been discussed interminably because of doubts about its author, its date, its connections with

8. Josephus Iscanus, *Werke und Briefe*, Ludwig Gompf, ed. (Leiden and Köln: E. J. Brill, 1970).

Vergil, and its derivation or nonderivation from a Germanic poem.[9] Only rarely have questions been raised about its structure. Its language clearly owes much to Vergil's *Aeneid* and other Latin works, such as the *Psychomachia* of Prudentius, but its structure is independent of them. The conflict between the hero and the king could hardly be more explicit. Waltharius is a hostage at the court of Attila and, although he is well treated and actually commands the king's forces in a defeat of the Pannonians, he is unhappy and determined to escape. His method is interesting. He creates chaos at the court by getting the king and his nobles drunk at a feast celebrating his own victory on the king's behalf and flees with his betrothed and a large treasure while the members of the court are unable to follow him. We see the pattern intruder-hero/defeat of weak king. The subsequent action is a little more complex. Waltharius intrudes into the lands of King Gunther (Guntharius) quite by accident. He has no designs on his lands and would prefer to pass through peacefully, but he cannot escape the epic structure. His intrusion is made very clear by the incident of the "Danube fish" with which he pays the ferryman. It denotes the man from another country, and Gunther is informed. This act of informing the king of the presence of an intruder and hence of danger is particularly characteristic of Germanic epic. It occurs in *Beowulf*, the *Nibelungenlied*, and the Dietrich epics as well as here and offers some evidence that the author may well have known of a German poem in which the motif was found.

An intruder was always potentially dangerous and he had to be watched and, if possible, interrogated about his intentions. Since Waltharius is alone, except for Hiltigunda, his betrothed, the danger is clearly small, and Guntharius moves swiftly to take advantage of the situation. He hears of the treasure and demands that Waltharius give it—and Hiltigunda—to him in exchange for peaceful passage. The challenge by Guntharius constitutes a reversal of the normal situation, in which the intruder-hero challenges the king, and it happens because Waltharius is alone and

9. *Waltharius*, Karl Strecker, ed. (2d ed.; Berlin: Weidmann, 1924).

Guntharius is foolish as well as being weak. Hagano warns him of the danger of challenging a warrior of Waltharius' prowess, but the king fails to grasp the quality of the man he is challenging. Here, as in the *Nibelungenlied*, it is Hagano who shows sense and who, in the end, saves his master from total disaster. Waltharius defeats all the warriors sent against him in a day-long series of combats, whose variety must have delighted the many connoisseurs of battle scenes among the readers of the poems. The next day Hagano allows himself to be persuaded that he should join Guntharius in an attack on Waltharius, but the outcome is far from favorable to the king. He is much more gravely wounded in the combat than the other two and is furthermore disgraced and ignored when Waltharius and Hagano celebrate their reconciliation.

The relationship of a weak king, Guntharius, and a powerful and sensible Hagano is essentially the same as that in the *Nibelungenlied,* that is, the southeastern version of the conflict between Siegfried and the Burgundians and between the Burgundians and Attila. Yet the hero is Waltharius and he is shown first as a highly successful "exile" at the court of Attila and then as an unwitting intruder into the territories of Gunther. The king reacts in the manner of a king in epic, who is something less than noble yet believes he must react in epic fashion to the intruder and pays the penalty. *Waltharius* is an artificial epic, very probably an attempt by a cleric to show that a Germanic story could be rendered in Vergilian form, and it is, therefore, all the more interesting that the theme of weak king and hero-intruder should remain so much a part of the poem.

Up to now we have been discussing epics which have some relationship to the Greek classical tradition, even though the connection may be no more than an attempt to imitate Vergil's Latin diction. *Beowulf* is a work of a completely different kind. It is the earliest complete Germanic epic and the only one written down at a period not totally remote from the period of the Germanic migrations. Whatever evidence there is of influence from Christian sources or from classical epic, the work remains essentially pagan in its ethic and in its views of the relation of the individual to his fellowmen and to society. The form, too, owes little or nothing to the classics. It is written in a verse-form peculiar to the Germanic peoples, and its metaphoric structure finds parallels only in the Norse Eddas and lyrics and Anglo-Saxon lyrics and epic fragments.[10]

Although it is never advisable to forget that even the earliest form of a written epic may be markedly different from its numerous oral predecessors, there is good reason to assume that *Beowulf* demonstrates many of the features which are to be regarded as characteristic of Germanic epic. What is perhaps even more significant is the evidence of conscious manipulation of those characteristics by the author of the extant version. Whatever one's views on two- or three-part structure, there can be little doubt that the author intended to depict the young Beowulf and the old Beowulf, Beowulf the intruder-warrior and Beowulf the settled king, declining King Hrothgar and rising warrior Wiglaf. The poem thus offers a study of the rise and fall of man and the rise and fall of rulers and hence of society. This interpretation is confirmed by the numerous citations of analogous events from other societies.

The author makes admirable use of the theme of conflict between the hero-intruder and the king. The poem, after a brief introduction of Hrothgar, King of the Danes, telling of his ancestry and of how he attained his present position as a respected and civilized king, draws a picture which is totally at variance with the concept of a successful ruler. The mead-hall, the center of light and civilization, is not controlled by its founder and lord but by an intruder, Grendel. We never find out exactly what Grendel is. He walks on two legs, has hooks of steel in his hands and scales for skin (984, ff.). He is a monster but a monster who

10. Ursula Dronke, ed., *The Poetic Edda* (Oxford: Clarendon Press, 1969), vol. 1, *Heroic Poems*; Patricia Terry, ed. and trans., *Poems of the Vikings* (Indianapolis: Bobbs-Merrill, 1969).

is an aberration from the human race, not a beast or a devil. As we find out later, his element is submarine and hence he intrudes not only upon the mead-hall but upon the terrestrial world of humanity.

Grendel exemplifies the intruder at his worst, a person possessed by evil, who cares only to destroy everything which civilization and religion have created and to bring death wherever he goes. Nevertheless, this monster is, when the poem opens, the true lord of Heorot. He has driven Hrothgar and his followers from the hall. They are scattered in outbuildings and deprived of their heritage.[11]

> Þā wæs ēaðfynde   þē him elles hwǣr
> gerūmlīcor   ræste [sōhte],
> bed æfter būrum,   ðā him gebēacnod wæs,
> gesægd sōðlīce   sweotolan tācne
> healðegnes hete;   hēold hyne syðþan
> fyr ond fæstor   sē þǣm fēonde ætwand.
> Swā rīxode   ond wið rihte wan,
> āna wið eallum,   oð þæt īdel stōd
> hūsa sēlest.   Wæs sēo hwīl micel;
> twelf wintra tīd   torn geþolode
> wine Scyldinga,   wēana gehwelcne,
> sīðra sorga; (138–49)

(Then someone could easily be found who looked for his rest somewhere farther off, for a bed in an outbuilding, as soon as the hate of the hall-thane became as clear as a beacon and was truly told. Anyone who escaped from the enemy kept himself farther off and more secure after that. So Grendel dominated and gained against the right, one against all, until the best of houses stood empty. Thus it was for a long time; for twelve long winters the court of the Scyldings suffered miserably every kind of sorrow and enormous grief.)

Many men have perished in Grendel's attacks, but Hrothgar is not one of them. He has not been able to save his hall or his men from the intruder nor has he sacrificed his life for them. Pleasant

---

11. Frederick Klaeber, ed., *Beowulf and the Fight at Finnsburg* (3d ed.; Boston: Heath, 1950).

though he is and generous as he proves to be, he has failed in the primary duty of a king. He cannot defend his people. The evil intruder has triumphed.

> Swā ðā mǣlceare   maga Healfdenes
> singāla sēað;   ne mihte snotor hæleð
> wēan onwendan; (189–91)

(So Healfdene's son kept brooding over his misery. Wise though he was, the hero could not turn the sorrow aside.)

It is important that the opening scenes should be viewed in this way. The apparently firmly established and certainly civilized rule of Hrothgar has been wrecked, the kingdom of the Danes has been handed over to the forces of evil, and Hrothgar himself, in spite of pomp and circumstance, is a king in name only. Beowulf is an intruder of a different kind. He has chosen to challenge the intruder who has taken charge but he does so with a degree of formality which is in sharp contrast with the behavior of Grendel. He is a well-known warrior in his own country, but there are hints that he feels a need to prove himself.

> Hēan wæs lange,
> swā hyne Gēata bearn   gōdne ne tealdon
> nē hyne on medobence   micles wyrðne
> drihten Wedera   gedōn wolde; (2183–86)

(But he was humiliated for a long time when the sons of the Geats thought him no good, and the lord of the Weders had no desire to grant him much honor at the mead bench.)

His followers are few and they constitute no threat to the kingdom of Hrothgar. Nor are they of any significance in the story. Unlike Grendel, Beowulf approaches from the sea, like many normal intruder-heroes. His coming is perceived by a coast watchman, and the subsequent behavior on both sides shows how well fixed were the conventions concerning the arrival of the intruder-hero. Beowulf is courteous in his reply to the guard's request for information, identifies his race and origin but does not immediately tell his name. He does praise Hrothgar and explain that he has heard of his troubles and has come to offer his help (267 ff.). All this is done without boasting and it could, of course, be no more than a prelude to an attack, a fact which does not escape the watchman. He courteously offers to escort Beowulf and his men along the highroad to Heorot but with equal courtesy proposes to leave a guard on their ship to protect it against raiders. The guard serves equally well to prevent the new arrivals from leaving if there is any reason for detaining them.

On arrival at the palace, Beowulf and his men pile their arms, again an act of courtesy indicating the absence of any hostile intent, but they remain alert. The second recognition scene follows a similar formal pattern. A nobleman asks who they are, so that the king may not be insulted by having dangerous or unworthy persons brought before him (333 ff.). The "recognition nobleman" or a similar character is to be found in most Germanic epics, and his role is often of much greater importance than it is in *Beowulf*. It is of most significance in the person of Hagen in the *Nibelungenlied*. The nobleman's interest is in the reason for Beowulf's voyage. His remark that he is "sure that it is due to daring and a spirit of adventure not because of exile or banishment" (337 ff.) reveals that he is, in fact, far from sure and that the two latter are the reasons for most of the arrivals of foreigners. Beowulf does no more than state his name and that of his lord but the nobleman, Wolfgar, is apparently satisfied, for he urges Hrothgar to receive Beowulf (366 ff.). This intervention of the nobleman protects the king both from physical danger and from the shame which might result and thus preserves the dignity of kingship. After this highly conventional reception of Beowulf, it proves that such precautions were not necessary. Hrothgar knows of Beowulf and greets him warmly. It is quite clear that the author's purpose is to contrast Beowulf's arrival with that of the normal intruder-hero, who poses real danger to the king whose territory he enters.

The danger would be all the greater because of the precarious hold Hrothgar has on his domain. His failure to protect his hall against Grendel clearly proves that he is now an inefficient king, however attractive he may be personally. Such a king is clearly ripe for replacement by a younger, more effective man. Beowulf is such a man. Yet the story does not develop in this way. Beowulf vanquishes Grendel within Heorot and he does so without arms. The rejoicing of Hrothgar and his followers is premature, as might be expected of a group which had lost touch with the reality of the impact of evil on human society. They were unaware of the existence of Grendel's mother and the evils beneath the mere, for the simple reason that they had never left their comfortable hall to find out. When Grendel's mother brings back to Heorot the chaos of the Grendel domination, Hrothgar and his followers are again plunged into despair. Only Beowulf retains his composure and good sense. He follows the blood-tracks to the mere but there is little or no support for him when he leaves his own element to challenge Grendel's mother in hers. His victory owes nothing to Hrothgar and his court or even to his own followers. He wins by his personal strength and fortitude and by a marked element of good fortune. The court which has totally failed to support him again breaks into enthusiasm and overloads him with lavish gifts and even more lavish praise (1700 ff.).

There is a good deal of evidence that Hrothgar is afraid of the consequences of Beowulf's success. He rewards Beowulf lavishly but he is eager to see him go back to his homeland:

> Đū scealt tō frōfre   weorþan
> leal langtwīdig   lēodum þīnum,
> hæleðum tō helpe. (1707–09)

> (You shall become a solace for a long time to your people, a help to heroes.)

The greatness of Beowulf lies in the fact that he acts in precisely the opposite fashion to that to be expected of an intruder-hero who has demonstrated unmistakably the weakness of a king and his failure as shepherd of his people. Beowulf could easily have taken over but he has too much sense of nobility, of the fitness of things, of the need to preserve kingship rather than destroy it, to take advantage of the situation. He leaves Hrothgar apparently secure in his kingdom, but the audience has been told, even before Beowulf's arrival, of the ultimate destruction of Heorot by fire, and further details are given. It would clearly have been in the interest of Heorot if Beowulf had taken over. Even later, when an opportunity presents itself to take over the kingdom of the Geats during the minority of the legitimate heir, he refuses and acts only as regent (2369 ff.). His concern for legitimacy is commendable, but there is a great deal of evidence that it is ineffective as a policy. The heir is as rash as his father and even less successful as a ruler. Only when Beowulf himself succeeds to the kingship, in legitimate succession, is peace finally assured and kingship secured.

> þǣr him Hygd gebēad   hord ond rīce,
> bēagas ond bregostōl;   bearne ne truwode,
> þæt hē wið ælfylcum   eþelstōlas
> healdan cūðe,   ðā wæs Hygelāc dēad.
> Nō ðȳ ǣr fēasceafte   findan meahton
> æt ðām æðelinge   ǣnige ðinga,
> þæt hē Heardrēde   hlāford wǣre,
> oððe þone cynedōm   cīosan wolde;
> hwæðre hē hine on folce   frēondlārum hēold,
> ēstum mid āre,   oð ðæt hē yldra wearð,
> Weder-Gēatum wēold.
>   Hyne wræcmæcgas
> ofer sǣ sōhtan,   suna Ōhteres;
> hæfdon hȳ forhealden   helm Scylfinga,
> þone sēlestan   sǣcyninga
> þāra ðe in Swīorīce   sinc brytnade,
> mǣrne þēoden.   Him þæt tō mearce wearð;
> hē þǣr [f]or feorme⁻   feorhwunde hlēat,
> sweordes swengum,   sunu Hygelāces;
> ond him eft gewāt   Ongenðīoes bearn
> hāmes nīosan,   syððan Heardrēd læg,
> lēt ðone bregostōl   Bīowulf healdan,
> Gēatum wealdan;   þæt wæs gōd cyning. (2369–90)

(Thereupon Hygd offered him treasure and kingdom, rings and the throne. She did not trust her son's ability to hold the ancestral seat against foreigners now that Hygelac was dead. But even in their wretchedness they could not prevail upon the hero to be Heardred's lord or to take over the kingdom; on the contrary, he gave him friendly counsel before the people, with goodwill and honor, until he grew older and ruled the Weder-Geats.

The sons of Ohthere, banished men, sought him out from beyond the sea; they had rebelled against the lord of the Scylfings, the best of the sea-kings who distributed treasure in Sweden, a famous prince. That brought about Heardred's life's end; in return for his hospitality the son of Hygelac received a mortal wound, a sword stroke. After Heardred was dead, the son of Ongentheow [Onela] went back to his homeland and allowed Beowulf to keep the throne and rule the Geats. He was a good king.)

The second part of the work is carefully designed to present a situation similar to that of the first part but with the key roles played by Beowulf reversed. Instead of being the intruder-hero, he is now the aged king. But he is not Hrothgar. To him the defense of his people is his prime concern. There is no mention of a hall like Heorot or of any center of light. Beowulf the king concentrates on the virtues of the warrior. The peace of the kingdom is disturbed by an intrusion of a strange kind. A slave within the territory enters a cave which is part of that territory geographically but not temporally. It is full of treasures from an earlier world and protected by a dragon whose sole reason for existence is to guard that treasure and prevent it from being employed for any useful purpose. The slave is hardly the normal hero-intruder, but the result of his theft of a cup from the dragon's hoard is to loose the violence of the dragon on Beowulf's domain.

It is clear that this time the intrusion is from inside and has no constructive intent. The dragon is bent on destruction, but is is a destruction for revenge, not for the gaining of fame or power (2302 ff.). Nevertheless, the challenge to Beowulf is the same as if an intruder had invaded his kingdom from the sea. He must defend his people and he must defend his right to the kingship, and to him the former is much more important than the latter.

There are none of the formalities we observed when Beowulf approached. The only question is how the violence of the dragon shall be counteracted, and there is a sharp contrast between the preparations of intruder-hero Beowulf and Beowulf the aged king. It will be remembered that he used no weapons against Grendel and that the sword he took down with him into the mere proved useless. His body was protected only by a corselet; there was no mention of a shield. Against the dragon Beowulf concentrates on defense. He orders a special shield to be prepared, heavily faced with iron, so that he may protect himself against the fiery breath of the monster. The shield proves to be as ineffective as the sword lent by Unferth had been against Grendel's mother.

> him ðæs gūðkyning,
> Wedera þīoden   wræce leornode.
> Heht him þā gewyrcean   wīgendra hlēo
> eallīrenne,   eorla dryhten,
> wīgbord wrætlīc;   wisse hē gearwe,
> þæt him holtwudu   he(lpan) ne meahte,
> lind wið līge. (2335–41)

> (For that the war-king, lord of the Weders, planned revenge. The protector of warriors, commander of nobles, ordered a fine shield to be made for him, all of iron. He knew full well that a shield of wood could not help him against the flame.)

The author seems intent on proving that weapons, whether offensive or defensive, do not win combats. They are decided by personal qualities and by fate. The dragon is defeated and killed, only partly by Beowulf. All of Beowulf's men flee in terror except Wiglaf, who stays to help his king and survives the battle.

It might be thought that the author of the poem was here offering a solution to the problem of succession in kingship. The aged ruler, fully conscious of his responsibilities but no longer physically capable of fulfilling them, is aided in his last, glorious fight against evil by a young warrior who has chosen himself by his

courage in remaining to face the dragon. There is no question
here of an incompetent ruler's being replaced by an intruder-hero.
The solution is attractive, but the conclusion of the poem hardly
seems to demonstrate that the author believed it would work. The
end is full of foreboding, and Wiglaf is unable to carry out Beowulf's wish that the treasure be distributed, that is, put to practical
use. It is once again buried and thus lays up for the future the
same problem of hoarding and obsession with mere control of
wealth which caused the dragon's wrath.

> 'Ic ðāra frætwa   Frēan ealles ðanc,
> Wuldurcyninge   wordum secge,
> ēcum Dryhtne,   þē ic hēr on starie,
> þæs ðe ic mōste   mīnum lēodum
> ǣr swyltdæge   swylc gestrȳnan.
> Nū ic on māðma hord   mīne bebohte
> frōde feorhlege,   fremmað gēna
> lēoda þearfe,   ne mæg ic her leng wesan (2794–801)

(For these treasures which I see here I give thanks in words
to the lord of all, the king of wonders, the eternal ruler and
that I was able to win such for my people before my death's
day. Now that I have given the late years of my life's span
for this treasure hoard, watch over the people's needs in the
future. I can stay no more.)

Beowulf the poem examines the problem of kingship and
succession through the life of Beowulf the man. It shows that
every kingdom needs a ruler who is aware of the first duty of a
king, the protection of his kingdom against intruders. Hrothgar
had once had this knowledge and power but he had lost it because
of an obsession with what we may call the material and esthetic
aspects of kingship. He is fortunate indeed that the intruder-hero
Beowulf not only carries out the duty of killing Grendel and his
mother, themselves intruders, which he should have fulfilled himself, but also that Beowulf is too noble to profit from his superiority at Hrothgar's expense. By contrasting Beowulf's conduct
with that of the violent intruder, the author stresses his hero's
exceptional quality and Hrothgar's good fortune.

In the long run, Heorot cannot be saved. Internecine struggles will destroy it and it is not by any means certain that Beowulf's kingdom was not destroyed in a similar way. Beowulf has no trouble with the intruder from outside. It is the opponent from within who destroys him, and this opponent is the personification of wealth hoarded and not used for encouraging bravery and good conduct, as Hrothgar, to his credit, had used his. Avarice is the weakness of aging men, and the author may wish us to understand that it is not merely against outside forces that a king must contend. Even Beowulf, the ideal hero and king, is not fully proof against the vice of avarice, and his dying wish to see the treasure distributed may reflect his repentance.

The structure of *Beowulf* is apparently based on the knowledge that its contemporary audience would recognize the conflict between settled king and intruder as the norm of epic poetry and would be able to appreciate the various ways in which the theme is introduced and, in particular, the contrast between the abnegation of Beowulf, the intruder-hero, and his counterparts, whose aim is to destroy.

Although there are probably four centuries or more between the composition of *Beowulf* and the traditional date of the composition of the *Nibelungenlied* (1203), it is sensible to consider the German work next. The immense amount of secondary literature devoted to its origins, its connections with Norse materials on similar themes,[12] and its role as "the" Germanic epic have tended to obscure the important fact that the extant versions were composed at a time when the epic was an ancient, even obsolete form. The dominant narrative genre in Germany at the beginning of the thirteenth century was the romance, and its values informed all the poetry of the courts. The stories of Siegfried and the Burgundians were, to put it least offensively, un-

---

12. Its subject matter is essentially Germanic and is closely connected with stories in the verse and prose *Eddas*, the *Thidrekssaga*, and the *Völsungasaga*.

fashionable, and were probably regarded by many as crude and unworthy of serious literature.

The author of the *Nibelungenlied* was fully aware of the dominance of the "courtly" viewpoint and makes great use of it in his work. The young Siegfried is knighted, and the celebrations include jousting. He goes to the court of Worms because he is determined to win Kriemhilde, his *amor de lonh*, whom he has never seen.[13] Nor does he see her for a long time at Worms but remains faithful and "serves" for her by aiding her brother Gunther to win his own *amor de lonh*, Brunhilde. After his death, Kriemhilde remains totally faithful to his memory, even after she marries Attila. The work has thus many of the common features of courtly poetry. The problem we have to solve is how seriously to take the use of such courtly characteristics and how they are to be reconciled with the totally different ethic presented by the poem as a whole. The application of the motif of conflict between king and intruder-hero is of considerable value in helping us to understand what the author intended.

The first intrusion in the *Nibelungenlied* is that of Siegfried at Worms. His stated intention is to go there to seek the hand of Kriemhilde. He is warned that Gunther, her brother and the king of the Burgundians, and Hagen, his principal retainer, are fierce and that his reception will be hostile. He remarks that he will take their lands and people from them in that case. It should be remembered that at this point in the narrative, the reader might be excused for thinking that Siegfried was a young, raw, and untried warrior who would be destroyed by the Burgundians. Such opinions are soon proved wrong. Siegfried's arrival at Worms is presented, quite deliberately, with all the conventions pertaining to the intruder-hero. He is accompanied by only twelve warriors—a retinue, not an army—quite insufficient for an assault

13. Jaufre Rudel, in his lyric "Lanquan li jorn" provides the first extant example of the use of the term "far-off love." *Les Chansons de Jaufré Rudel*, Alfred Jeanroy, ed. (2d ed.; Paris: 1924). The author of the *Nibelungenlied* chooses to interpret the expression in terms of physical distance, although it is unlikely that it was so intended by Jaufre.

on the kingdom. They are magnificently equipped and attract everyone's attention, so that Gunther wishes to know who they are.

The parallels with the situation in *Beowulf* are obvious and these continue when Hagen is called in to identify the strangers. A history of Siegfried's exploits is provided which is quite inconsistent with what the reader had been told earlier but very much in conformity with the picture of Siegfried as it is given in other epic and poetic sources. We are told of his defeat of Schilbung and Nibelung and acquisition of their treasure, and of the attempt of the dwarf Alberich to avenge his masters and of his subsequent swearing of fealty to Siegfried. In the course of these events, Siegfried obtained the cloak of invisibility and later, by bathing in the blood of a dragon he had killed, he acquired invulnerability. (Hagen apparently does not yet know of the vulnerable spot.) All of these are features of epic poetry, not of romance, and they are exactly what would be expected of the arrival of the hero-intruder. Here is a man to strike fear into any court, and the king and his advisers will have to decide what attitude to take toward him. There is clearly the hope that he will prove amenable if treated gently, and the fear that he may be aggressive and overthrow the ruler. It is the classic dilemma at the arrival of the intruder. It may also be noted that the reaction of the court is to Hagen's story, not at this time to Siegfried himself.[14]

Gunther is perfectly courteous in his reception, but Siegfried immediately issues a challenge which incorporates the worst fears of the Burgundians. He has come to wrest from them their lands and possessions.

> "Nu ir sît sô küene,   als mir ist geseit,
> sone ruoch' ich, ist daz iemen   liep oder leit;
> ich wil an iu ertwingen   swas ir muget hân;
> lant unde bürge,   daz sol mir werden undertân."

14. It can be argued that most of the action in the *Nibelungenlied* springs from the reactions of characters to the myth or at least the reputation of other characters.

Den künec hete wunder   und sîne man alsam
um disiu maere   dier hie vernam,
daz er des hete willen,   er naeme im sîniu lant.
daz hôrten sîne degene;   dô wart in zürnen bekannt.

"Wie het ich daz verdienet",   sprach Gunther der degen,
"des mîn vater lange   mit êren hât gepflegen,
daz wir daz solden vliesen   von iemannes kraft?
wir liezen übele schînen   daz wir ouch pflegen riterschaft."
(110–12)[15]

("Even if you are as bold as I have been informed, I don't
care who likes it and who does not, I intend to take by force
whatever you may have; your lands and castles are going to
be subject to me."

The king was amazed—and so were his men—at the statement he had just heard, that Siegfried intended to take his
lands away from him. His warriors heard it and felt their
anger rise.

"How have I deserved," said the warrior Gunther, "that we
should lose what my father long cared for in honor to someone's strength? If we did, it would give a poor impression of
the kind of knighthood we practice.")

This is the challenge of the intruder-hero in the crassest possible
form and, not unnaturally, Hagen and, even more, Ortwin are
stung and eager and ready to take up the challenge. Calmer coun-
sels prevail, and Siegfried's mood of boasting and challenge
passes quickly away and never reappears. The author says that
it was the thought of Kriemhilde which restrained him (the only
reference to her at this stage), but it seems much more likely that
he is showing the "romance" Siegfried of Xanten trying to behave
like an epic intruder-hero at Worms. In other words, Siegfried
resented the implication in the speeches of his parents that the
warriors at the court of Worms were too powerful for him to
challenge and he therefore arrives there in the role of what he

15. *Nibelungenlied*, Karl Bartsch, ed. 13th ed., Wiesbaden: Brockhaus, 1956).

considers to be the epic intruder-hero. His behavior is thus designed to bolster his own conception of himself.

From the point of view of the ethic of the poem, the contradiction in the behavior of Siegfried is even more important. It is never possible to be sure whether this warrior, the greatest in the northwest Germanic tradition, is really what tradition says he is and what he imagines himself to be or whether he has been corrupted by the ethic of the romance and is concerned not with the great political questions of kingship and public policy but only with individual prowess and fame and the winning of his lady by love-service. The author has thus used the conventions of the arrival of the hero-intruder very cleverly by showing his hero as conscious of what such a person should do in these circumstances and then as exaggerating that behavior almost to a parody. One might almost say that Siegfried had heard too many epics.

The next example is even more interesting. The intrusion is made this time by a king, Gunther. Siegfried accompanies him, and Brunhilde is told that he is a mere liegeman. In fact, the intruder is again Siegfried. It is he who performs the tasks set and deposes the queen, thus fulfilling the role of the successful intruder-hero, so far as Brunhilde is concerned—and at the same time performing a kind of love-service to win Kriemhilde. The conditions of the expedition are peculiar. Gunther does not depart in search of power or plunder but to win a bride and is thus acting in the same manner as Siegfried had earlier in the poem. The purpose is that which we would expect to find in a romance or in an even cruder *Brautwerbungsgeschichte* (bride-quest story), but the methods are those of an epic. Brunhilde is to be won not by love-service but by individual combats in which sheer strength will be the deciding factor.

The actual journey displays the usual conventions—selection of the group, in this case only Gunther, Hagen, Dankwart, and Siegfried, provision of clothing, described at unusual length because the object was to win a lady, and a brief description of the actual voyage. Until the landing itself there is little that is unusual in the description of the intruder, but as the four approach Brunhilde's domain, the conventions are flouted and flouted with a purpose. It is not warriors they see but ladies standing in the window, and Gunther is asked by Siegfried which he would choose. He correctly picks Brunhilde, but the interesting point is that Siegfried knows her by sight. We never discover how he knows her, but the parallel with Hagen's recognition of Siegfried, although he has never seen him, is clear. No warriors put on armor to receive the party, but ladies put on finery and it is they, not warriors, who discuss the new arrivals. When they are admitted, the stacking of arms by courtesy which we observed in *Beowulf* is replaced by a demand that the Burgundians give up their arms. Hagen objects. He is used to the epic tradition. Here the conflict works by artificial rules—as it would in a romance.

It is of course, Brunhilde, a woman, who asks who these warriors are and it is ladies who reply. They do not know any of the men personally but *believe* that one is Siegfried. The others are nobles conventionally described—except for the emphasis on the fierce looks of Hagen. Brunhilde assumes at once that it is Siegfried who has come to challenge her and says that she will not yield to him without a fight, even if he is Siegfried. Thus she accepts that there is a challenge by an intruder-hero, a challenge which will, according to the rules, bring death to all the intruders or the marriage of Brunhilde to one of them. Her kingdom as well as her person will pass into the hands of the victor and she will no longer be an independent queen. Brunhilde had devised the tests and the fearsome penalty for failure to ensure that she would lose her royal power and her virginity only to the bravest and strongest of men. The challenge to the settled ruler thus has features which are very significant. The challenge is not, as it usually is in epic poetry, entirely of a political nature. Here it is the loss of independence as a woman which accompanies loss of royal power. The woman goes the same way as the queen. The struggle that follows thus contains elements of both the epic and the romance inasmuch as the challenged ruler is a woman who, allegedly, is being sought more for her beauty than for her realm and political power.

The first meeting between the ruler and the challenger is an interesting and deliberate distortion of the intruder convention. Brunhilde asks Siegfried the conventional question: "What is the purpose of your visit?" (Interestingly, she addresses him as Siegfried without further inquiry.) She receives a quite unconventional answer. Siegfried refers her to Gunther and adds that he would not be in Island were he not there as Gunther's liegeman. The challenger is thus introduced at second hand and he does not speak until both Siegfried and Hagen have had their say. Even then he merely states his intention, a bold declaration very much at variance with the terror shown by both him and Hagen when they see Brunhilde, fully armed with her enormous shield and spear. Yet this same mighty warrior is described as dressed in rather flamboyant but unmistakably feminine fashion, in silk decorated with gold bars and with a shield-strap of green silk studded with gems. Although the two contestants go through the motions of three epic tests, the real contest is invisible, since it is really between Brunhilde and Siegfried. The element of parody remains as strong as ever. In a contest between ruler and intruder, the victory is won by an invisible man, a third party who wins for another. Kingship is lost by the incumbent but not gained by the true winner. A woman is betrothed to a man who has not won her.

The transfer of power is effected only when Siegfried fetches his own men to ensure that the challenging parties have really the power to overcome the forces of Brunhilde. The epic convention reasserts itself, but the winning of Brunhilde is another matter. The romance convention would certainly not tolerate a situation in which a lady once won would refuse to consummate a marriage. Brunhilde's refusal to do so stems from the very conditions she had set to safeguard her virginity and her royal power. They have been fulfilled, but she cannot believe that there is not something suspicious, since the idea of defeat had never occurred to her. Siegfried's forces clinch the transfer of power, but she is determined to test the validity of the trials by refusing to consummate the marriage in a manner most humiliating to Gunther. She thus transfers the epic power contest to the man-woman relationship which should be settled in terms of the romance. The consummation of love is effected in the most violent physical terms. The alleged intruder-hero is totally defeated, and the substitute hero again subdues the bride so that consummation can take place. On both levels, the political and personal, the intruder-hero fails and yet wins by the intervention of a more powerful helper. The epic and romance conventions have both been distorted.

The intrusion into Worms by Siegfried and by Gunther and Siegfried into Island has produced the desired result: Siegfried has gained Kriemhilde but there has been no transfer of power; Gunther has gained both Brunhilde and her kingdom but both by deceit and on false pretenses. Kriemhilde and Siegfried live as they would in a romance, Gunther and Brunhilde live discontented and with friction. The intrusions that follow all stem from these two states of mind. When Siegfried and Kriemhilde return from Xanten to Worms, it is by invitation, in other words exactly the reverse of the action of an intruder-hero. In fact, however, there is a challenge. Brunhilde invites them for one purpose only. She desperately wishes to prove the subservience of Siegfried to her husband and what purports to be an invitation is, in her eyes, a command. The first meeting of the two queens is deliberately described as a festival in the romance manner, and the theme of romance, as opposed to epic, conventions is continued when the two queens are described as sitting together watching warriors practicing knightly exercises:

> Vor einer vesperzîte   huop sich grôz ungemach,
> daz von manigem recken   ûf dem hove geschach.
> si pflâgen ritterschefte   durch kurzewîle wân.
> dô liefen dar durch schouwen   vil manic wîp unde man. (814)

> (Before the time of vespers a great disturbance arose caused by many warriors at court. They were practicing knightly exercises to pass the time. Many women and men went there to look on.)

The mixture of terms is interesting. The men are "recken" (epic)

but they are engaged in "ritterschaft" (romance) "durch kur-
zewîle" (romance). The two women are watching as Guenevere
or Soredamors might have done, but their behavior is totally
different from that of their romance counterparts. They do not
discuss, nor are they interested in the prowess of the warriors.

Kriemhilde opens with a totally unprovoked and totally unmotivated statement that she has a husband good enough to rule
any kingdom in the world. The challenge is clear and it is the
female counterpart of Siegfried's equally unmotivated challenge
earlier in the poem. Brunhilde finds herself in the position of
Gunther. She, who had brought Kriemhilde here to test her, now
finds herself in the position of the challenged ruler. She hardly
knows what to say or how to act. She has to defend the superiority
of Gunther, in which she does not really believe, and finally allows
herself to be lured into a status competition of dress and finery
which she cannot win and which has as little to do with the relative
merits of Gunther and Siegfried as a victory by Lancelot has to
do with the chastity of Guenevere.

> "Du ziuhest dich ze hôhe",   sprach des küniges wîp.
> "nu wil ich sehen gerne,   ob man den dînen lîp
> habe ze solhen êren   sô man den mînen tuot."
> die vrouwen wurden beide   vil sêre zornec gemuot.
>
> Dô sprach diu vrouwe Kriemhilt: "daz muoz et nû ges-
>   chehen.
> sît du mînes mannes   für eigen hâst verjehen,
> nu müezen hiute kiesen   der beider künige man,
> ob ich vor küniges wîbe   zem münster türre gegân.
>
> Du muost daz hiute schouwen,   daz ich bin adelvrî,
> unt daz mîn man ist tiwerr   danne der dîne sî.
> dâ mit wil ich selbe   niht bescholten sîn.
> du solt noch hînte kiesen   wie diu eigene diu dîn (826–28)
>
> Ze hove gê vor recken   in Burgonden lant.

("You are setting yourself too high," said the king's wife.
"Now I am determined to see whether your person is held

in such honor as mine.'' Both the ladies were now very angry indeed.

Then the lady Kriemhilde said: "That shall be now. Since you have declared my husband to be a bondsman, the liegemen of the two kings shall choose today whether I am permitted to go into the minster before the king's wife. You shall see today that I am a free noblewoman and that my husband is rated more highly than yours is. I am determined not to be insulted in this. You are going to have the chance this evening to witness this your bondswoman walking to court in front of the warriors in the land of the Burgundians.)

The author has cleverly transferred the epic contest between the king and the intruder-hero into feminine terms, a contest where Kriemhilde brands Brunhilde with the ultimate insult— *kebse* or whore—and defeats her by wearing the girdle and ring taken from Brunhilde by Siegfried. Like all the other features of this contest, the evidence gives a totally false impression. Brunhilde is as deceived by Kriemhilde as she was by Siegfried but she has received one piece of true information which confirms her worst fears. It was Siegfried who defeated her, as she had suspected, but he is married to another woman.

Gunther accepts Siegfried's word that he had never boasted of having taken Brunhilde's virginity. In this, as in everything, he is the *roi fainéant*. It is Hagen who listens to Brunhilde's complaint and who destroys Siegfried. The two streams of epic and romance thus merge. The original challenge made by Siegfried and so resented by Hagen and Ortwin has not been forgotten. Siegfried's increasing domination of the court at Worms and his performing for Gunther tasks which Hagen could not have undertaken, have led to bitter resentment. Here, at last, is the chance to revenge them and to do so in a manner befitting a person to whom his king was sacrosanct. Yet the actual quarrel is nothing more than a squabble between two women about social status and precedence. The courts of Worms and Xanten, the homes of epic heroes, are having their lives—and, as events prove, their destruction—put at the mercy of women. The romance convention that the conduct of knights is determined entirely by the wishes of ladies is carried to its logical conclusion in a context that is entirely epic. The male intrusions in search of a female which characterized the first part of the epic and which inevitably led to the epic power challenge have been replaced by female intrusions whose result is death.

Siegfried dies at the hands of Gunther for two reasons. He has been the ultimate cause of an insult to Brunhilde which can be wiped out only in blood. He pays the penalty for his wife's behavior, as a romance hero should. But the other reason, though less obvious, is more important. Hagen sees Siegfried as a constant danger to the Burgundian court, to King Gunther, and not least to himself. His utterances make this perfectly clear:

> Sîn gevolgete niemen,   nîwan daz Hagene
> riet in allen zîten   Gunther dem degene,
> ob Sîfrît niht enlebte,   sô wurde im undertân
> vil der künege lande,   der helt des trûren began. (870)

(No one supported him in this, except that Hagen kept on urging the warrior Gunther on every occasion that if Siegfried were to die, many of the king's lands would fall subject to him. The king began to get very gloomy about this.)

He is concerned with problems of power and thinks in terms of the use of power, however brutal, for gain. He destroys Siegfried as one destroys an animal. There can be no question of combat, epic or chivalric, since Siegfried would be bound to win. Hagen, logical in this as in all things, is prepared to throw all epic conventions of honor and all romance conventions of chivalry to the winds. Siegfried must be removed by any possible means. He therefore plays upon his victim's foolish egoism and is able to lure him to his own destruction, an animal among animals. His remark over the dying Siegfried reveals his motives:

> Dô sprach der grimme Hagene;   "jane weiz ich waz ir kleit.
> ez hât nu allez ende   unser sorge unt unser leit.
> wir vinden ir vil wênic,   die türren uns bestân.
> wol mich deich sîner hêrschaft   hân ze râte getân." (993)

(Then the grim Hagen said: "I don't know what you are complaining about. All our misery and sorrow is now over. We shall find very few people who dare resist us. Good for me that I have put a term to his domination.")

He has removed a rival and a threat, and there should be no sentimental heroics.

There is again a period of relative calm. Hagen logically deprives Kriemhilde of Siegfried's treasure to prevent her from conspiring against her brothers, and he strongly, though vainly, opposes her marriage to Etzel. Although it would be straining structural credulity to describe the arrival of Rüdeger at Worms as the arrival of an intruder-hero, it is worth noting that he is faced with a challenge—persuading Kriemhilde to marry Etzel—and that he wins, as he thinks, by swearing an oath always to defend her. His ethic, attuned to thinking of women in romance terms, fails to grasp the uncompromising pusuit of revenge which is characteristic of the epic. He is to pay dearly for his confusion.

After consolidating her position at Etzel's court, Kriemhilde invites her brothers and Hagen there. The parallel to the invitation to Siegfried by Brunhilde is clear, but whereas Brunhilde had merely wished to test her suppositions, Kriemhilde is consciously plotting the destruction of the Burgundians. They arrive by invitation, but Hagen, again personifying the epic convention, regards his voyage as that of an intruder-hero. Although the Burgundians are ostensibly going to visit Etzel and the sister of their king, Hagen thinks in terms of a coming struggle. The effort to find out the future from the merwomen and his subsequent ruthless test of the accuracy of their predictions by his attempt to drown the chaplain both point to his conviction that the visit will be a trial of strength.

There will not, of course, be a direct individual combat between Kriemhilde and a warrior, nor will there be the war of words that occurred between Brunhilde and Kriemhilde. This confrontation will be, if Hagen can arrange it, a struggle between all the forces the Burgundians can muster and all those whom Kriemhilde can persuade to fight for her. Hagen, alone of the Burgundians, realizes the immense hold which her love of Siegfried still has on Kriemhilde. He knows because he has the same intense feeling about the maintenance of Burgundian kingship. The most powerful epic motivation, loyalty to one's liege-lord, will face the most powerful romance motivation, loyal and enduring sexual love.

Before the arrival of the Burgundians at Etzel's they have spent an idyllic four days at the court of Rüdeger. This interlude is the passage in the poem which is closest to a genuine romance incident. The young Giselher, by far the most attractive and chivalrous of the Burgundians, is betrothed to Rüdeger's daughter and even Hagen is close to behaving in a style befitting a civilized court. Only his tactless request for a shield that had belonged to a dead kinsman of Gotelind, Rüdeger's wife, spoils his record. The arrival of the Burgundians at Bechelare is observed by women, not warriors, and their departure, with gifts, is accompanied by women. There is such sharp contrast with normal epic arrival and departure, and still more with the theme of intrusion and challenge, that it must be assumed that it has been inserted by the author as a deliberate and antithetical prelude to the arrival of the Burgundians at Etzel's court.

It is also no accident that Kriemhilde, like Brunhilde in Island, is at a window waiting for her kinsmen to arrive. She, too, expects a challenge, but her motives are very different. Before they arrive, however, news of their approach is brought to Dietrich and he goes to warn them of their danger from Kriemhilde who, as he says, still weeps for Siegfried. This action constitutes a most interesting reversal of the normal role of the nobleman guarding the court which we saw in *Beowulf*. Dietrich has no need to ask the Burgundians who they are or what the purpose of their visit is. He attempts to use the occasion against the wishes, if not the best interests, of his liege-lady. Gunther cannot understand why a warning should be necessary, Hagen has no wish to heed it. In spite of the fact that their identity is known, the courtiers are anxious to see what Hagen looks like and, although the reader is well acquainted with him already, a further description follows. It is extremely significant that the curiosity is about Hagen. Gunther is, after all, the king, but it is Hagen who is not only the intruder but the person who is to challenge Kriemhilde. By making him the object of the conventional curiosity about the intruder-hero, the author indicates very clearly the true nature of the arrival of the Burgundians and of the challenge to come.

The challenge begins, as it is destined to end, with a question from Kriemhilde. Where is the Nibelungen treasure which rightly belongs to her? Hagen's reply is insulting, and he adds to the insult by referring to the arms he is wearing. Kriemhilde is quite right when she says that he should not be wearing them and particularly should not be carrying his sword—or rather Siegfried's—in the king's hall. But Hagen, who had, although unwillingly, agreed to give up his weapons at Brunhilde's court, here contemptuously refuses to do so. There could be no better indication of his changed role. In Island he was obliged to conform to a set of artificial rules because his lord wished to win Brunhilde, and only Siegfried, not he, could ensure that the king succeeded. At Etzel's court he determines the rules of the game because he alone of the Burgundians realizes what the game is.

His statements to Kriemhilde also reveal a most important split in the forces at Kriemhilde's disposal. Dietrich not only admits that he had warned the Burgundians of their danger but virtually asks his liege-lady what she proposes to do about it. She is too afraid to take any action. This extraordinary behavior of Dietrich serves two purposes. It dissociates the greatest hero of the southeastern Germans from subservience to a foreign queen, one whose motivation was not a desire for revenge for the death of a blood kinsman but a determination to murder, as the older tradition saw it, blood kinsmen to repay them for the killing of her lover. It further explains why Dietrich allows the whole sorry chain of events to take place when it is clear that he could have defeated the Burgundians at an early stage. If he had done so, and thus acted as a true supporter of Etzel, he would have helped

Kriemhilde to achieve her purpose, with which he does not agree. His tragedy is that, in preventing her success, he destroys friend and enemy alike.

When Hagen's direct challenge comes, it is of a personal nature which well suits the situation. There is no challenge to Etzel, the ruler. Hagen lays Siegfried's sword across his knees as Kriemhilde passes by with a large escort. Not only does he insult her by remaining seated but he calls her attention to the fact that her dead husband's sword is in his possession.

> Der übermüete Hagene   leit' über sîniu bein
> ein vil liehtez wâfen,   ûz des knopfe schein
> ein vil liehter jaspes,   grüener danne ein gras.
> wol erkandez Kriemhilt,   daz ez Sîfrides was.
>
> Dô si daz swert erkande,   dô gie ir trûrens nôt.
> sîn gehilze daz was guldîn,   diu scheide ein porte rôt.
> ez mante si ir leide;   weinen si began.
> ich waene ez hete dar umbe   der küene Hagene getân.
> (1783–84)

(Hagen was defiant and laid across his legs a brightly shining weapon from whose pommel there shone a brilliant jasper, green as grass. Kriemhilde recognized at once that it was Siegfried's. When she recognized the sword, the wretchedness of her loss came upon her. The hilt was of gold, the scabbard a red orphrey. It reminded her of her misery and she began to cry. That, I think, was the reason bold Hagen did it.)

It is as if he had conquered Siegfried in battle, but the implication is as false as that of Siefried's possession of Brunhilde's ring and girdle. Hagen has no hesitation in admitting responsibility or in pointing out to Kriemhilde that it was her insult to Brunhilde which brought about Siegfried's death. He thus makes his actions the subject of personal enmity between himself and Kriemhilde, and she must choose a champion to avenge her wrongs. There are many similar situations in the romances. Kriemhilde must now try to persuade or bribe individuals and groups from Etzel's entourage to act as champions for her. There is no question of a threat to the king's power. This is purely a situation where a lady seeks champions to avenge her lover but in doing so she wishes to prove what she has said to Brunhilde—that he was the greatest of men and others must yield to him, even in death. Her determination to carry this conviction to its utmost conclusion destroys the forces of Etzel and Dietrich as well as all the Burgundians.

The author demonstrates very well how Hagen's insults to Kriemhilde, including the unprovoked murder of Etzel's son by her, and her own obsession with revenge gradually draw into the conflict even those whose convictions are far removed from the cause for which they are ultimately called upon to fight. There are two tragic examples, both apparently the invention of the *Nibelungenlied* poet. Rüdeger, the Christian gentleman, to whom an oath and his personal morality are of supreme importance, finds himself forced by his oath to defend Kriemhilde against the Burgundians, whom he admires and one of whom is to become his son-in-law. He is totally opposed to Kriemhilde's purpose but he is bound not only by his rash oath to her but by his duty to Etzel. When he tries to obtain the king's leave to withdraw from his obligations, he finds that his lord is kneeling to him, begging for help. The world has been turned upside down, and Rüdeger perishes in the conflict.

Etzel der rîche   vlêgen ouch began.
dô buten si sich beide   ze füezen für den man.
den edelen marcgrâven   unmuotes man dô sach.
der vil getriuwe recke   harte jâmerlîchen sprach.

"Owê mir gotes armen,   daz ich ditz gelebet hân.
aller mîner êren   der muoz ich abe stân,
triuwen unde zühte,   der got an mir gebôt.
owê got von himele,   daz mihs niht wendet der tôt! (2152–53)

(Now powerful Etzel began to entreat him too and both fell at the feet of their own liegeman. There the noble margrave was seen in confusion. The most loyal warrior spoke in profound misery: "Alas, godforsaken as I am, that I should live to see this. I must give up all my honor, my loyalty, and my principles which by the grace of God I possess. Alas, God in Heaven, why does not death save me from this?")

Dietrich, as we saw, warned the Burgundians of the intentions of Kriemhilde. He, too, is bound to Etzel by strong ties, since the king had given him an honorable refuge in exile. For as long as he can, he evades his obligations. To him the Burgundians are honorable men who are being destroyed by a vengeful woman. Only after all his men have been destroyed under the leadership of Hildebrand, while trying to avenge the death of Rüdeger, does Dietrich enter the fight against Gunther and Hagen, the lone survivors. After capturing them, he begs Kriemhilde for their lives. His plea is vain. She has Gunther executed and strikes down Hagen with her own hand. This sequence of events is illustrative of the author's interpretation. As we noted, it is Hagen who is the real intruder and Kriemhilde who is the true ruler, and the conflict is between them. In physical terms, Kriemhilde wins, since she kills Hagen with her own hands and with Siegfried's sword, but in death he defeats her completely by his refusal to tell her where he has hidden the treasure. The moral victory is his and even her physical victory is short-lived. Hildebrand, horrified that a great hero should die at the hand of a woman, cuts her down.

The *Nibelungenlied* is a series of deliberate perversions of the theme of the conflict between the hero-intruder and the settled king. It begins with a true hero (Siegfried) and a true king (Gunther), but the encounter between them is little more than a charade, for Siegfried is merely attempting to establish an image of himself which inspires fear, since, as he believes, he must impress Gunther and Hagen in order to win Kriemhilde. The second contest is between a king posing as an intruder-hero (Gunther) against a settled ruler, Queen Brunhilde. Here again the contest is a charade, for the real competitors are Siegfried and Brunhilde, and again it is for a woman, the ruler herself. Neither of these two contests is overtly about power, as a true

contest between hero-intruder and king should be. In fact, however, they both bring great influence to Siegfried, who dominates
the Burgundian king, and also bring on him the fatal jealousy of
Hagen. Burgundian kingship suffers but so does the kingship of
Brunhilde, sacrificed to the wrong intruder.

Women are concerned in both conflicts, indirectly in the first,
directly in the second. It is logical, therefore, that the third confrontation should be between two females and that it should determine the fate of all the major characters in the poem. Kriemhilde, the invited intruder, challenges the ruler to combat over
precedence. The men are merely witnesses in the battle, not
participants. Kriemhilde wins the battle of precedence but in
doing so destroys her husband. Brunhilde succeeds in vindicating
her position as ruler by forcing Gunther to agree to Siegfried's
destruction but in doing so she ultimately brings about the destruction of the whole Burgundian power. The last conflict is
between Hagen and Kriemhilde and it is, finally, a struggle for
power. Hagen must show that Kriemhilde cannot destroy Burgundian kingship, Kriemhilde must humiliate the murderers of
her husband.

The basic perversion in all these episodes is the introduction
of women acting as do the ladies of the romance. As one episode
succeeds another, it is more and more women who are making
the vital decisions, and their obsession with their personal values
and particularly sexual love, leads to wholesale destruction, not
only of themselves and the men closely connected with them but
also of men like Rüdeger, whose only wish is to observe the
highest moral standards. It is fitting that the supreme confrontation in the work should be between Hagen, the highest personification of the values of the heroic epic, and Kriemhilde, the
personification of unlimited power put in the hands of a woman.

For there seems little doubt that the author of the *Nibelungenlied,* by these perversions of the basic theme of epic poetry and
particularly by making these perversions so largely the result of
the interference of women, wished to contrast the values of the
epic and the romance, in a manner very much to the disadvantage

of the latter. For him, society could continue to exist only if kingship were wielded by great men guided by a sense of public duty. The only true reality was power in the hands of a king, and the only true duty of a subject was to make sure that that power was maintained. The interference of women in this power structure is fatal, particularly if their conduct is guided by personal considerations and by love for a husband rather than a blood kinsman. When the romance concept that a court should be dominated by women and by their concepts of morality is pushed to its logical conclusion and allowed to dominate the behavior of men, the result can only be chaos and the total destruction of values. There can be no such theme as the confrontation between the hero and the queen.

The *chanson de geste* presents many difficulties to the student of epic poetry. Not the least of these is that numerous representatives of the genre are extant, so that we are not in the position of having to judge a form from one or two examples, as we are in studying early Greek or early Germanic epics. These representatives are by no means homogeneous in style and some are clearly no more than imitations or extensions of earlier works which had gained success. A further complication is introduced by the fact that a large number of the epics can be ascribed to one of two cycles, the cycle of the king (that is, of Charlemagne), and the cycle of revolted barons.

Each of these two cycles shows a markedly different ethos. Those of the Charlemagne cycle lay great stress on loyalty to a noble king, who is God's vicegerent on earth and who, whatever temporary weaknesses he may display, must finally triumph and be worthy of the confidence of his peers. In the other cycle the king is weak, even shifty, incapable of carrying out effectively the duties of his office and, worse still, incapable of distinguishing between the loyal hearts whom honesty compels to tell him unflattering truths and the servile courtiers who are interested only in self-promotion.

It will be noted that the two cycles present the two images of the king which we have been discussing and that they are both much concerned with the behavior of noblemen under the conditions we have mentioned. There is in all of them an element which has not been of any real significance in any of the works already discussed, that of Christianity. The morality of the earlier epics is social, although supported by a framework of religion. There is no question of one religious belief being right in itself and conferring on its believers a privileged status, so that actions they perform in its name have greater validity if they are good or pardon if they are bad, whereas the same actions performed by nonbelievers are condemned.

The introduction of Christianity into epic poetry means that the actions of participants are no longer judged only by their effect on the social and political fabric within which the characters move but by reference to their effect on the salvation of the individual soul and the triumph of the Church. The situation is not made easier by the fact that the earlier, probably oral, form of these epics, although composed in a period nominally Christian, was concerned much more with the facts of the narrative, briefly told, and with simple morality. The Crusades and theological justification of them in the late eleventh and the twelfth centuries, as well as the pretensions of some twelfth-century rulers to theocratic kingship caused a revision of the works and the attitude which informed them.[16] Charlemagne became more than a great organizing Christian king; in the epics he was *the* Christian, *the* emperor, and his empire was synonymous with *Christianitas* (Christendom). His battles are not merely against his own enemies but against the enemies of God. Glory and fame are not the only or even the principal spur. He must continue to fight

16. Gaston Paris, *Histoire poétique de Charlemagne* (1865), rev. ed Paul Meyer (Paris: E. Bouillon, 1905); Paul Lehmann, *Das literarische Bild Karls des Grossen*, Sitzungsberichte der bayerischen Akademie der Wissenschaften, phil.-hist Klasse, 9 (1934); K. E. Geith, *Carolus Magnus: Studien zur Darstellung Karls des Grossen in der deutschen Literatur des 12. und 13. Jahrhunderts, Bibliotheca Germanica* 19 (1977).

God's battles until the last enemy is destroyed. From this it follows that anyone who opposes the Emperor or who obstructs his success in the name of personal glory or personal vengeance is acting against God's purposes for the world and is worthy of condemnation.[17]

The poems of the cycle of the king thus raise difficulties which do not appear in studying earlier epics. The *Chanson de Roland*, by far the best of them and, so far as can be determined, the earliest extant shows these difficulties most clearly and a discussion of it illuminates the problem. Let us point out first of all that there is more than one *Chanson de Roland*. The Oxford Digby version is the best known and unquestionably superior to the others as a work of art, but it should not be forgotten that it stresses the personality and role of Roland far more than other versions. Perhaps the most significant difference between the Oxford version and the others, including those in German and Norse, is that the former shows a real conflict between Charlemagne and Roland, whereas the latter never waver in depicting the Emperor as the unshakable Christian champion whose difficulties are brought about by the sins of his men.

The *Chanson de Roland* in the Oxford version is organized as a series of confrontations.[18] These take various forms, of which the simplest is armed combat. Many of the confrontations are internal, that is to say, they concern members of the same side and, curiously enough, there are far more of these dissensions among the Christians than among the pagans. The poem opens with a significant juxtaposition, a *laisse* (poetic paragraph) about Charlemagne the Emperor, followed by one about Marsile. This opposition remains an essential feature of the structure of the poem. The pagan council shows remarkable accord in sending

17. In the *Historia Karoli Magni et Rotholandi ou Chronique du Pseudo-Turpin*, Cyril Meredith-Jones, ed. (Paris: Droz, 1936) a clear connection is made between the sins of Charlemagne's men and the subsequent defeat.

18. *Chanson de Roland*, Joseph Bédier, ed. (Paris: H. Piazza, 1947; frequently reprinted). I have used the Bédier text, with its modern French translation, because of its wide accessibility, but see also Aurelio Roncaglia, ed., *La Chanson de Roland* (Modena: STEM Mucchi, 1947), with other relevant texts.

the peace mission to Charlemagne. Blancandrin offers advice and Marsile takes it, but the purpose is evil and unity alone does not demonstrate that a cause is just. At the Christian court the situation is totally different. Charlemagne holds a formal council after he has heard the pagan proposals and puts them to his barons. They are suspicious. According to custom, every baron, like his counterparts in the *Iliad*, is entitled to express his opinion about the way in which proposals should be treated. It is the way in which this council is handled in the poem which shows that here too we are faced with the conflict between the hero and the king. Roland wastes no time in leaping to his feet and stating his views. He clearly is suspicious of the pagans' intentions but much more important is his *gab*:

Je vos cunquis e Noples et Commibles,
Pris ai Valterne e la tere de Pine
E Balasgued e Tuele e Sezilie (198–200)

(I have conquered for you Noples and Commibles, I have taken Valterne and the land of Pine and Balaguer and Tudela and Sezilla.)

He continues with an account of an earlier example of Marsile's treachery. The most important feature of his speech, however, is Roland's claim that he is responsible for victories Charlemagne has won.

This is, of course, the typical action of the intruder-hero. He is brash, challenging, and makes extravagant claims for himself without regard to political and social consequences. His reason for wishing to continue the war is entirely personal, the hope of acquiring still greater glory, and this concern with fame continues to motivate his conduct almost to the hour of his death. An outburst of this sort in epic poetry should call forth a rebuke, preferably from the king himself, but if not, from another noble. The reaction to Siegfried's outrageous challenge will be recalled. The reply in the *Chanson de Roland* comes from another noble, Ganelon. He accuses Roland of pride in opposing the peace proposals and of lack of interest in the welfare of the emperor's subjects:

> "Ki ço vos lodet que cest plait degetuns,
> Ne li chalt, sire, de quel mort nus muriuns
> Cunseill d'orguill n'est dreiz que a plus munt;
> Laissun les fols, as sages nus tenuns!" (226–29)

> (". . . anyone who advises you, sire, to reject this accord is little concerned, with the kind of death we die. It is not right that advice which springs from pride should prevail. Let us abandon the fools and stay with the wise!")

The reply is accurate and describes perfectly the attitude of the self-centered hero as contrasted to the responsible king. The weakness of Ganelon's position is that his speech is inspired not by concern for the emperor or his subjects but by jealousy of Roland. His words, however, convince the Duc de Naimes and through him, the rest of the barons. Roland has urged the right course, the only one which would be possible for a dedicated Christian emperor, the complete destruction of the pagans but he has done so for the wrong reasons, since his only concern is personal glory. The "reasonable" course, also urged for the wrong reasons, has triumphed.

From the point of view of epic tradition, the most important feature of this scene is the behavior of Charlemagne. In history and in epic he should listen to the opinions of his barons but give a firm decision himself. We have pointed out the failure of kings in epic to reach decisions when faced with the truculence of an intruder or opponent and the dire consequences which spring from the failure. Here the decision is simply not made explicitly. Charlemagne does not comment on the speeches of either Roland or Ganelon. He merely asks, "Whom shall we send to Saragossa?" He thus tacitly accepts the advice of Ganelon. He is wrong to do so, for in taking the line of least resistance he is directly responsible for the later tragedy. It will be observed how the standard epic pattern is modified by the impact of Christianity. Instead of an intruder-hero who moves in from outside to challenge the authority of a king, on purely personal grounds or with the object of achieving power and status, we have an internal conflict in which the personal ambition of the hero is opposed to the emperor. The decision goes against the hero because the emperor is weak in the sense that he does not recognize his duty. Roland is thus the instrument of God in calling for unremitting war against the pagans, even though, as an individual, he is guilty of pride in placing his own interests before those of *Christianitas*. Ganelon, who in terms of epic structure is the supporter of the ruler and the opponent of the intruder-hero, and hence the supporter of the establishment, proves to be the most destructive force in the poem. There is thus established a tension between heroic epic and Christian order which continues through the work.

The tension persists into the next episode, the selection of an ambassador. The offer by the Duc de Naimes to go is refused by Charlemagne. Roland's offer is also refused, but the interesting point is that it is opposed by Oliver, Roland's friend (255 ff.). The reason is clear: Roland would behave at the court of Marsile as he had already done at the court of Charlemagne and disturb the "reasonable" negotiations which are to take place. The "reasonable" person, Ganelon, is chosen, against his will, because he is proposed by Roland, again from spite and again without any positive decision from Charlemagne. Although Roland has virtually mocked Ganelon, and although Charlemagne has been made aware of the bitter feud between the two, he selects Ganelon as his ambassador.

> Ço dist li reis: "Guenes, venez avant,   AOI
> Si recevez le bastun et la guant.
> Oït l'avez, sur vos le jugent Franc."
> "Sire," dist Guenes, "ço ad tut fait Rollant!" (319–22)

> (Then the king said: "Ganelon, step forward and take the staff and the glove. You heard, the Franks have chosen you." "Sire," said Ganelon, "this is all Roland's doing!")

Again the stress is on the weakness of the emperor and on his inability to make a decision in the Christian sense. He is as much a victim of intruders as Hrothgar and Gunther, since he is unable to make the decisions which alone would justify him as a ruler. He appoints Ganelon even when he hears how desperately Ganelon hates Roland and when his handing over of his glove is so obviously ill-omened. We are faced with the classic situation of the ruler unable to control a situation.

The visit of Ganelon to the court of Marsile again offers an interesting comparison with the corresponding epic situation. Ganelon is accompanied there by Blancandrin, as Beowulf was accompanied as he approached the court of Hrothgar, but there is no parallel to the treachery which is worked out on the way. Yet even this agreement does not prevent an act which would be perfectly normal in epic structure but which is totally out of place in the context of treachery. His delivery to Marsile of Charlemagne's terms is a mixture of bluster and threats of the most insulting kind (425 ff.). Marsile is on the point of throwing his javelin and Ganelon's sword is half out of its scabbard when the pagans intervene.

This kind of behavior would be very appropriate for an intruder-hero but not for an ambassador, especially one who is a traitor to his own cause. One explanation is that Ganelon is hiding his true feelings to make a good impression, but this argument could not apply to Marsile. It is far more likely that the incident is determined by the epic convention of boasting by the intruder. The resolution of their conflict is equally interesting. Marsile describes Charlemagne as decrepit, Ganelon as bold and strong, but both agree that Roland gives him his power (520 ff.). The plot thus tacitly recognizes that it is not the king who provides the strength of his kingdom but a subject, and both thus recognize the form of Christian rule which is at the heart of the poem. Further, Roland, Ganelon, and even the pagans contribute to the ultimate recognition by Charlemagne of the role he should play.

One of the features which should be noted at this point is the stress on material goods. In the epic tradition, the right to receive rewards is always important; the quarrel in the *Iliad* begins precisely as a result of such claims. Equally important was the right of a ruler to establish his reputation by the distribution of largesse, as a reward indeed but also as a demonstration of his own generous character.

This movement of treasure is invariably present in epic poetry. But how does it appear in the *Chanson de Roland*? The pagans move to the material question very early in their discussion of peace (*laisse* 3), and there is constant reference to quantities of gold, jewels, and fine cloth which will be sent as presents or rather bribes. Charlemagne mentions this wealth when discussing the proposals, but there is no evidence in the Oxford version that it plays any role in his decision or has influence on subsequent events. Its epic function is to characterize the pagans as obsessed with material goods and as unable to grasp the true function of gift-giving or rather as perverting it.

Again the importance of the Christian influence on the poem is evident—the contrast between the ideals of *Christianitas* and *Gentilitas*. The epic tradition as it appears in the *Iliad*, the *Aeneid,* and *Beowulf* finds nothing disgraceful in the search for and acquisition of material goods, either as prizes of war or as rewards for service. Indeed they play a major role in the relations between ruler and subject, king and warrior. This function rarely appears in the Oxford version. Charlemagne does indeed rejoice in the capture of Cordres with a great quantity of booty (*laisse* 8), but as a defeat for the pagans rather than as material acquisition. No mention is made of any division of the spoil.

Ganelon is definitely bribed by the pagans with large quantities of gold for himself and a precious necklace for his wife (617 ff.). There is no doubt that Marsile thinks that such a bribe can affect his conduct. Yet it is made abundantly clear in the poem that Ganelon needs no such motivation. His reason for attempting to destroy Roland and Oliver is personal hatred. Here, as elsewhere, the pagan obsession with material goods is contrasted with the Christian clash of personalities. The conflict before Charlemagne makes this perfectly clear.

It must be remembered that Ganelon's negotiation of an apparently honorable peace meets with the approval of almost all the army, that its terms are accepted without the slightest hesitation by Charlemagne, and that it is at this point in the poem that Charlemagne approaches most closely to the *roi fainéant* (698 f.). Like Hrothgar and Gunther, he allows events to take charge and, in particular, allows the natural desire of his troops to return home to override the judgment which he, as Christian emperor, should show in assessing the likelihood that the pagans will, in fact, follow him to Aachen and accept Christianity.

This same indecision leads to his second abnegation of responsibility. Ganelon, in accordance with his agreement with Marsile, proposes that Roland command the rear guard. There is nothing unusual or criminal about this suggestion. It accords well with the epic code of honor, and it would be hard for Roland to refuse. Indeed, it might be expected that Roland would ask for the post himself. Why, then, is Roland so angry:

> . . . Ireement parlat a sun parastre:
> "Ahi! culvert, malvais hom de put aire,
> Quias le guant me caist en la place,
> Cuma fist a tei le bastun devant Carle? AOI (762–65)

> (. . . he spoke angrily to his stepfather: "You villain, you wicked man of vile origin, did you think that I would let the glove fall to the ground as you let the staff fall in front of Charlemagne?")

The answer is that he suspects treachery, as Charlemagne had done.

> Quant l'ot li reis, fierement le reguardet,
> Si li ad dit: "Vos estes vifs diables.
> El cors vos est entree mortel rage." (745–47)

> (When the king heard this, he looked at him severely. Then he said to him: "You are a real devil. A fatal madness has entered your body.")

Yet nothing is done to change the situation. The quarrel between Roland and Ganelon, whatever its roots, is about to affect the whole Christian army and the success of Charlemagne's mission, and it is the emperor's duty to prevent the dreadful consequences.

His failure to do so shows that the destructive forces represented by Roland and Ganelon, each intent on personal glory, gain, or reputation have triumphed temporarily over the central idea of *Christianitas* represented by Charlemagne but not carried through because of the moral weakness of the ruler. It is worth noting that the anger of Achilles had, for most of the time-span of the *Iliad*, the same effect on the Greek cause and that Aeneas' involvement with Dido, in his intruder-exile phase, seriously prejudiced his mission to found Rome. Had Beowulf been of less sterling stuff, his personal ambition could easily have led to the premature end of Hrothgar's kingdom, a point which the author is at some pains to stress.

The long battle between the rear guard and the pagans, like that between Charlemagne and Baligant, is a shattering confrontation between the forces of good and evil and is intended to represent that struggle in striking terms, but in the structure of the epic the important motif is the working out of the conflict between personal honor and the support of a social order which is the essential problem of the hero. The conflict is polarized by opposing Roland, the representative of self-centered, "heroic," and destructive behavior, to Oliver, the reasonable, prudent, and socially minded representative of the establishment. The motivation of Roland's conduct of the rearguard action is the desire for personal glory. He has no doubt about his reason:

Respunt Rollant: "Jo fereie que fols!
En dulce France en perdreie mun los.
Sempres ferrai de Durendal granz colps;
Sanglant en ert li branz entresqu'a l'or." (1053–56)

....

"Ne placet Deu," ço li respunt Rollant,
"Que ço seit dit de nul hume vivant,
Ne pur paien, que ja seie cornant!
Ja n'en avrunt reproece mi parent." (1073–76)

(Roland replies: "I would be acting like a fool. I would lose my fame in sweet France. I shall keep on striking mighty blows with Durendal; its blade will be bloody from them right up to the gold hilt." . . . "May it never please God," Roland answered him, "that it should ever be said by a living man that I sounded my horn because of the pagans. Never may my kinsmen have to suffer disgrace from that.")

It is clear that Roland is concerned with one thing only, his reputation, and that the larger issues of the safety of his rear guard and the defeat of the pagans do not outweigh any threat to his personal prestige. Critics have laid much stress on Oliver's wisdom, as opposed to Roland's foolhardiness, but it is more relevant to the epic tradition to stress that Oliver is putting forward the views of the establishment.[19] Roland's view is precisely that of Achilles—that the preservation of the army to which he is attached and of the cause to which he is theoretically devoted is secondary to his own fame as an individual warrior.

Oliver's view is that of the king or, rather, what that of the king should be—that individual prowess and reputation, even individual honor, must be subordinated to the good of the general cause. In this case, it is not only the good of France but that of *Christianitas* which is at stake, and Oliver thus represents *sapientia* in the higher sense of divine wisdom. He is functioning in these scenes as the voice of God, ignored by Roland and unheard by Charlemagne. It might thus be argued that Oliver is at least as much a martyr as Roland, but the difference lies in the fact that Roland is a "convert" and Oliver is not. The ultimate confrontation is between a Roland who realizes his fault and an Oliver who is sufficiently deprived of his senses by wounds to reject Roland's reasonable attitude and see only the criminal obstinacy of his earlier behavior.

It should be noted that Roland's conversion is brought about not by an intellectual realization that he has failed the Christian cause and must attempt to make amends but by the heroic re-

19. See Brault (above, note 2), pp. 346ff, notes 75ff. for relevant literature.

lationship between friend and friend. Roland is affected by the fact that Oliver can no longer recognize the bond between them and indeed treats him as an enemy (1722 f; 1998 ff.). If such a thing can happen, the breach must be serious, and Roland is moved to understand the reasons for Oliver's conduct. His personal honor can now be concentrated on dying without shame, but he has been brought to recognize the folly of his earlier conduct. In other words he is now prepared to recognize that his personal honor should have been subordinated to the general welfare and that his conduct has been the direct cause of the death of his comrades. It is the sight of them lying on the ground which causes him to propose to Oliver that he now sound the horn for Charlemagne (1691 ff.), a decision based not on political calculation but on the sudden realization of the havoc his concern with personal honor has wrought. Oliver's reply is based on establishment considerations: there is now no question of recalling Charlemagne in time to rescue the rear guard and he is scornful of Roland's view that revenge is important:

> Dist Oliver: "Ne sereit vasselage!
> Quant jel vos dis, cumpainz, vos ne deignastes.
> S'i fust li reis, n'i oüsum damage. . . ." (1715-17)
> ....
> Ço dist Rollant: "Por quei me portez ire?"
> E il respont: "Cumpainz, vos le feistes,
> Kar vasselage par sens nen est folie;
> Mielz valt mesure que ne fait estultie.
> Franceis sunt morz par vostre legerie.
> Jamais Karlon de nus n'avrat servise.
> Sem creïsez, venuz i fust mi sire;
> Ceste bataille oüsum [faite u prise]. . . . (1722–29)

(Oliver said: "That would not be an act of real bravery. When I told you to do so, my comrade, you would not stoop to it. If the king had been here, we would not have suffered loss. . . ." Then Roland said: "Why are you angry with me?" And he replied: "My comrade, you brought it about. To behave sensibly with courage is not to behave like a madman. Self-

control is of more value than foolhardiness. The French have
died because of your irresponsibility. Charlemagne will never
have any service from us again. If you had taken my word,
our lord would have come; we would have fought and won
this battle.'')

Roland destroys himself in blowing the oliphant and thus in heroic
terms sacrifices himself to secure revenge. In Christian terms, he
martyrs himself for the Christian cause. Yet his motivation is not
Christian, and his abandonment of personal honor—in Christian
terms, *superbia*—is the result of an entirely epic consideration.
Roland, himself unwounded, sees that Oliver is mortally hurt:

Rolland reguardet Oliver al visage:
Teint fut e pers, desculuret e pale.
Li sancs tuz clers par mi le cors li raiet. . . . (1978–80)

(Roland looked at Oliver's face; dull and wan, drained of
color and pallid. The bright blood ran down the length of his
body.)

He weeps for France as much as for his friend, but the most
significant incident occurs when Oliver, no longer able to distinguish friend from foe, splits his helmet with a fierce blow:

A icel colp l'ad Rollant reguardet,
Si li demandet dulcement e suef:
"Sire cumpain, faites le vos de gred?
Ja est ço Rollant, ki tant vos soelt amer!" (1998–2001)

(At this blow Roland looked at him and then asked him quietly
and gently: "Sir, my comrade, did you mean to do that? It
is I, Roland, who loves you so much.")

Roland accepts the blow, not only without complaint but with
love, and they embrace. Roland's action is that of a Christian,
and he is now reconciled not only with Oliver but with *Christianitas* as represented by Charlemagne.[20] His subsequent actions

20. He is carrying out the Christian admonition to turn the other cheek (Matthew
5: 38).

are on its behalf, not for personal honor, as his treatment of Archbishop Turpin shows. Although when attempting to break his sword, Durendal, he again says that with it he has conquered many countries, he says he has done so for Charlemagne and emphasizes the religious aspects of his sword. His final act on making confession is to hold out his glove to God, the glove he had received with such wrath and, through the angel Gabriel, God accepts it.

Roland is thus converted from a self-centered, destructive hero, whose attitudes threaten both the emperor and *Christianitas,* to a fighter for the faith who dies a martyr. Yet the motivations of his conduct remain essentially those of the hero. His opposition to Charlemagne and Ganelon is based entirely on considerations of personal honor and his change of heart on pity for his comrades, particularly Oliver, and a desire for revenge on the pagans even at the cost of his own life.

We should now consider the conduct of Ganelon. It is too easy to regard him, as many versions of the story do, as an evil figure whose only concern is the destruction of Roland and, through him, of Charlemagne. Such an interpretation ignores the fact that he is described as noble, handsome, brave, and wise and, particularly, that a vast majority of Charlemagne's surviving nobles appear to be on his side at the trial. There can be little doubt that in the events preceding the opening of the poem he has been a loyal subject of Charlemagne's. What then is his motivation? Apparently he is not very far removed from Achilles, not in the sense that he has been deprived of a prize but because he feels that he has been wrongly treated. Roland's laughter and willingness, indeed eagerness, to send him on a dangerous mission clearly irritates old wounds. Roland is undoubtedly supercilious and arrogant, but the real problem is to be found in the opposition between personal and public considerations.

The trial of Ganelon, a carefully organized set piece, makes no attempt to obscure the fact that it is a portrayal of the struggle between the interests of the emperor, and hence of *Christianitas,* and those of individual nobles represented by Ganelon. The de-

fense is perfectly simple. Ganelon does not deny his enmity for
Roland or that he conspired to destroy him. He simply states that
the matter was entirely a matter of personal enmity and hence
not in the least treasonable:

> Dist Guenelon: "Fel sei se jol ceil!
> Rollant me forfist en or e en aveir,
> Pur que jo quis sa mort e sun destreit;
> Mais traïsun nule n'en i otrei." (3757–60)

(Then Ganelon said: "Shame on me if I conceal it. Roland
did me wrong in regard to my gold and my property. That is
why I sought his death and destruction; but I will not grant
that I committed any treason.")

He gives further details in his second exposition of his defense

> "Pur amor Deu, car m'entendez, barons!
> Seignors, jo fui en l'ost avoec l'empereür,
> Serveie le par feid e par amur.
> Rollant sis niés me coillit en haür,
> Si me jugat a mort e a dulur.
> Message fui al rei Marsiliun;
> Par mun saveir vinc jo a guarisun.
> Jo defiai Rollant le poigneor
> E Oliver e tuiz lur cumpaignun
> Carles l'oïd e si nobilie baron.
> Venget m'en sui, mais n'i ad traïsun." (3768–78)

("For the love of God, now listen to me, barons! My lords,
I was with the emperor and the army and I served him in
complete loyalty and affection. His nephew, Roland, hated
me and condemned me to death and sorrow. I was made
envoy to King Marsile. I saved myself by my own wits. Then
I challenged the bold Roland and Oliver and all their comrades. Charlemagne heard it and all his noble barons too. I
took my revenge, but there was no treason.")

The speech very carefully juxtaposes Ganelon's undoubted
services to Charlemagne and the Christian cause, including the

dangerous mission to Marsile, with his personal defiance of Roland. The last sentence sums up his view: "I took my vengeance, but there was no treason."

This defense epitomizes the essential struggle between hero and king, but here the basic theme is affected by two special, historical circumstances: the right of medieval and particularly Germanic noblemen to private feud, whether the sovereign agreed or not, and the belief that any action against Christianity in its fight against the heathen was in itself sinful and worthy of secular punishment, whatever the social justification might be. Medieval history is in many ways an account of the struggle of central authority to suppress private war, and the *Chanson de Roland* undoubtedly had a message for the nobles of the twelfth century, but from the point of view of epic construction the theme is unchanged, private honor against public policy.

We are never told what the causes are of the mutual hatred of Ganelon and Roland, but there is no reason to disbelieve Ganelon's account. He has a private feud with Roland and he uses the circumstances of the peace negotiations to bring about a solution. It is not hard to persuade the Saracen leadership that the destruction of Roland would deprive Charlemagne of his greatest asset and that therefore any sacrifice should be made to eliminate him and Oliver. Ganelon is thus using the political situation for personal revenge and furthermore manipulating it for that purpose. Achilles had done exactly the same, and it is possible that Turnus in the *Aeneid* is behaving in the same way. In all these cases the hero's course is destructive, based as it is on a personal, antisocial attitude. Ganelon is, in epic terms, no worse than these characters, and his behavior can be justified, but in terms of the Christian background which plays so important a role in all the Roland poems, he is not only an offender but a sinner. Much worse, he is careless not only of the secular power of his sovereign but of the whole of *Christianitas*.

The most significant indicator of the relation between Ganelon's conduct and Charlemagne's reaction is the attitude of the barons. In spite of the appalling losses to the army and the death of many friends, the barons are almost unanimously in favor of Ganelon. When the emperor looks for a champion to dispute his cause, he can find only Thierry, a person whose reputation as a fighter and whose appearance hardly inspire confidence that the cause will be justified. Again we have a common epic situation. The barons know that in supporting Ganelon they are laying up treasures for themselves. Their personal interests would be best served by a victory for the view that private feuds are possible even within the context of a major war and that the emperor must recognize a definition of treason that takes account of it. The corollary is that the emperor cannot claim that the interest of the state or, better, of the Christian community, override personal honor. Inevitably such a situation must lead to the disintegration of combined action against the heathen. "Heroic" action is shown once again to be inimical to a stable society, even though a majority of individuals may support it.

In the *Iliad*, the gods as a group have no policy. Aphrodite supports Troy, and Hera and Athena oppose it because of the Judgment of Paris. Other deities also take sides for what, in human terms, are personal considerations. Even Zeus himself is prejudiced in favor of Troy but neither he nor any other deity can interfere with fate. There is no evidence that fate is influenced by moral considerations in the sense of good or bad conduct by individuals. The rise and fall of states and kingdoms is decided by forces which even the gods can neither control nor understand. The obstinacy of Agamemnon and the self-centered pride and anger of Achilles provide the focal point of an epic struggle but they do not, in themselves, cause or prevent the fall of Troy.

The situation in the *Aeneid* is somewhat different. Although the Homeric framework is preserved, the power of Jupiter has been considerably increased, and it is made clear that his decision is the determining factor in the founding of Rome. Opposition by other deities, particularly Juno, is evidence of spite but can do no more than increase the hardships of the Trojan exiles. Aeneas is a more consciously moral person than Agamemnon, Achilles, or Odysseus, even than Hector and Priam, yet it is not his behavior but the will of Jupiter which leads him to Italy. Here, as in the *Iliad*, the viewpoint remains secular. The gods will not be disturbed by the outcome of events. There is no "good" side or "evil" side in the *Iliad*, and even in the *Aeneid* no evidence that those whom Jupiter allows to be destroyed are opposed to him or displeasing to him, still less that they are evil.

Quite the opposite is true in the *Chanson de Roland*. The contest is between God's forces and those opposed to him, and the only criterion of conduct is whether it supports the cause of Christianity or runs counter to it. There are, as we have seen, marked differences in character, not only among the Christians but among the pagans too. Many pagans are stated to be brave, handsome, and courteous. Yet their behavior cannot save them from damnation because of the cause they serve:

> Uns amurafles i ad de Balaguez;
> Cors ad mult gent et le vis fier e cler;
> Puis que il est sur sun cheval muntet,
> Mult se fait fiers de ses armes porter;
> De vasselage est il ben alosez;
> Fust chrestiens, asez oüst barnet. (894–99)

> (There was an emir there from Balaguer; his body was very handsome, his face bold and open. When once he was on horseback, he made a fine figure in his armor. He had a fine reputation for military prowess. If he had been a Christian, he would have been a true baron.)

Blancandrin falls into this category, and so does Baligant himself. Although the ultimate triumph of Christianity is assured in the light of God's providence, the behavior of individuals is to be judged by the contribution it makes to that triumph. Pagans, by definition, can make no such contribution, but Christians can also act against God's purpose if they allow considerations of personal honor or gain to make them act in a way detrimental to the triumph of Christianity. Here the introduction of the Christian/pagan opposition can complicate the epic opposition between the hero and the king. For the quarrel or conflict now becomes a question of a sin against a higher power, not merely a question of the priority of state policy as represented by the ruler over personal honor or material gain for the aggressive or intruding hero. A teleological element has been introduced which is totally foreign to the pagan epics. Roland's behavior, which would have been normal in a Germanic warrior, takes on a different complexion when seen as opposed to God, and it calls for expiation through martyrdom. Ganelon's conduct, understandable, permissible, and even laudable in a pagan society, becomes not only antisocial but antireligious in Charlemagne's *Christianitas* and must be expiated by a disgraceful death.

The judicial combat between Thierry and Pinabel which decides the major issue of the poem differs from such combats in other major epics in that protagonists are not involved. The question of the superiority of the hero or the king does not, therefore, arise and it is made clear that Thierry's victory is gained entirely by God's decision. Roland's death had been brought about by his own act in blowing the horn, an act of penitence. The larger issue is decided by God alone, for Thierry, although brave, was no match for Pinabel in purely physical terms. The climactic battle which we find in the *Iliad* (between Hector and Achilles), in the *Aeneid* (between Aeneas and Turnus), and in *Beowulf* (between the hero and the dragon) is not to be found in the *Chanson de Roland*. The battle between Charlemagne and Baligant settles only one issue, the defeat of a pagan force. It is stated in the last few lines of the poem that there will be other such confrontations. The major issue represented by both Roland and Ganelon, is whether private honor, private war, and private revenge have any place in a Christian world. It is God himself, through Thierry, who makes it clear that there is no such place, and the author, in telling us this, negates the whole ethical concept of a struggle between private honor and public policy which dominates epic poetry. But without that ethical concept the *Chanson de Roland* cannot be fully understood.

The unique nature of the *Chanson de Roland* appears when it is compared with the epics which make up the cycle of Guillaume d'Orange.[21] Here the conflict between king and hero could hardly be more explicit, and the sympathy of the composers of the epics is clearly with the hero. The confrontation between hero and king is depicted in the Guillaume cycle in a way which would be impossible in the *Chanson de Roland*. Louis is a weak king who nevertheless occupies the throne and therefore has at his disposal all the attributes of kingship, its powers of disposition of land and its demand for loyalty. It is kingship, not the king, which possesses these powers and it is to kingship, not the king, that Guillaume devotes his loyalty. Louis' behavior, as a person, is despicable. He fails totally to help his faithful liegeman; he awards him land which it is not in his power to grant. When Guillaume is defeated, he cannot help him. Yet Guillaume never fails to recognize the duty he owes. Because Louis is king, Guillaume must support him.

What is more significant in their relations is the fact that the king is poorly advised by courtiers who dislike Guillaume's direct methods and vigorous action. The king's weakness and timidity make him an easy victim of their intrigues and cause him to send Guillaume into virtual exile. After the series of defeats and the death of Vivien, Guillaume is left entirely to his own devices by the court and saves himself by his own exertions and the tenacity of his wife, Gybourg. There is thus a totally different level of conflict between hero and king in the Guillaume cycle.

The hero has no desire to press his claims to personal honor against the wishes and interests of his lord. On the contrary, he feels that his own activities should depend on and be coordinated with the king's. It is the failure of the ruler to respond to the demands of sovereignty which brings about conflict, and even

21. *Le Couronnement de Louis*, Ernest Langlois, ed. (2d ed. revue, Paris: Champion, 1961); *Le Charroi de Nîmes*, Duncan McMillan, ed. (Paris: Klinck-sieck, 1972); *La Chanson de Guillaume*, Duncan McMillan, ed. (2 vols.; Paris: A. & J. Picard, 1949–50); *Les Redactions en vers de la Prise d'Orange*, Claude Régnier, ed. (Paris: Klincksieck, 1966); *Aliscans*, G. Rolin, ed. (1897; rptd. Wiesbaden: Sändy [1967]). Useful English versions: Glanville Price et al., *William, Count of Orange: Four Old French Epics* (London and Totowa, N.J.: Rowman and Littlefield, 1975); Joan M. Ferrante, *Guillaume d'Orange: Four Twelfth-Century Epics* (New York: Columbia University Press, 1974).

then, Guillaume has no quarrel with the idea of kingship or with Louis as its personification but only with the bad advisors and with the policy they advocate. The epic cycle thus presents the paradoxical picture of hero and king in conflict for the king's own good. All the stress is on the actions of the hero, not only because he is exciting, vigorous, and intensely physical but because he is carrying out two roles, that of the individual in search of fame and that which should fall to the king, the prosecution of public policy by the defeat of the enemies of the realm.

This type of conflict becomes very common in twelfth- and thirteenth-century epics. The failure of a ruler to behave like a ruler was the haunting fear behind medieval public policy, and the numerous epics showing a king, in spite of himself, saved from bad advice and weak character by a hero who in part usurps his functions, testify to the concern over a *roi fainéant*. Guillaume's actions, as the poet depicts them, are principally concerned with his own fame. Much more time is devoted to detailed descriptions of his prowess in combat and of the sheer animal aggressiveness of his personality than to the motivation of his acts. There is no parallel in the *Chanson de Roland* to Guillaume's feuds with Acelon or Duke Richard the Red. Certainly these are enemies of the king, but it is much more important that they are enemies of Guillaume.

It is always dangerous to consider different poems in the same epic cycle in the chronological order of the events which occur in them, but there is a consistency in the relations between Guillaume and King Louis which invites a study of the progress of the king's treatment of his subject and Guillaume's reaction.

The *Couronnement de Louis* opens with Charlemagne's presentation of his son Louis to an assembly of nobles, an occasion of great solemnity and deep significance for the future of the realm. The king lays down rules for the behavior of a monarch, rules which would be universally regarded as valid, and demands that his son accept them before he is admitted to sovereignty. When Louis hesitates, more from timorousness than disagreement, Charlemagne is furious and is on the point of agreeing with a suggestion made by Arneis of Orléans that he should act as king for three years. Thus the poem begins with the actions of a scheming nobleman who attempts to take advantage of regal weakness.

The issue is settled by the crude intervention of Guillaume. For some reason he has decided to go hunting rather than attend this solemn ceremony but he now storms in and, without making any inquiry into the rights and wrongs of the matter, kills Arneis with his bare hands and himself sets the crown on Louis' head. Thus behavior of the crudest kind on the part of the hero ensures the succession and shatters a courtiers' plot. There is no reason why Guillaume's intervention should take the form it does unless we assume that the author was following a convention of such behavior by the hero and had deliberately kept him away from the original assembly in order to contrive his "rescue" of Louis. His actions are well received by Charlemagne, who proceeds to give further advice to his son including, significantly, an admonition not to trust lowborn people with power. Unfortunately Louis proves quite incapable of acting on his father's advice.

Guillaume goes on a pilgrimage to Rome and while there undertakes action against the Saracens on behalf of the church. Then he hears that Louis, now king, has been driven off his throne by a conspiracy of Richard, Duke of Normandy, and that he has taken refuge with an abbot at the church of St. Martin. Guillaume returns, assembles an army, and makes himself known to Louis, who virtually grovels at his feet. Guillaume takes action—against clerics, bishops, and citizens.

His treatment of the rebel Acelin, Richard's son, demonstrates so many features of the intruder-hero's behavior that it almost amounts to a parody of the motif. Guillaume sends a noble messenger, Alelme, to announce his support for Louis. His reception by Acelin is the mixture of arrogance, bravado, and attempted bribery which was noted in the mission of Ganelon to the Saracen court. Guillaume then confronts Acelin in person, is received with scorn, and, when threatened, springs the ambush he has set. Acelin's forces are destroyed, and Guillaume personally dashes out his brains with a stake.

After this episode of crude violence, Guillaume defeats Acelin's father, Richard of Normandy, and hands him over to Louis. Louis is thus restored to his throne, but it has been made painfully obvious throughout that he rules by the grace of Guillaume, that he is a nonwarrior who should get himself tonsured and live as a monk with the churchmen who protected him. The contrast between the ebullient hero, rejoicing in his strength, and the timid occupant of the throne is too crass to provide any real tension between hero and king.

Even when back on his throne Louis is too feeble to take determined action and he begs Guillaume to save him from enemies external and internal.

Guillaume is disgusted and has no hesitation in criticizing his sovereign and calling him coward and weakling. Yet he supports him and is in effect regent for several years. Like Beowulf, he recognizes the weakness of the king but never dreams of supplanting him. To Guillaume, the divinity which hedges a king is such that he must support even such a feeble occupant of the throne as Louis, a man who, unlike Hrothgar, had never shown that he was capable of ruling.

His loyalty is tested even more in the *Charroi de Nîmes*, for, as the last lines of the *Couronnement* predict, Louis shows no gratitude, and when Guillaume understandably storms into the king's presence and asks for a grant of land for his many services, his lord can do no more than offer him fiefs unjustly taken from good men or their heirs. Although there is no physical violence, there is a bitter verbal confrontation, and it is clear that we have a situation very similar to that in the *Nibelungenlied* in which Siegfried challenges Gunther in his own palace. It ends with Guillaume's obtaining from a reluctant Louis permission to take over lands now held by pagans. The king is giving away none of his possessions but he is clearly afraid of the consequences of annoying the pagans who hold the lands. It will be noted that the author never shows Guillaume attempting to take from Louis anything which belongs to him, including the throne. Yet he is perpetually confronting either his sovereign or, more frequently, that sovereign's courtiers. The motif of the intruder-hero is thus carefully modified to show Guillaume as a faithful liegeman.

Guillaume leaves the court, and once again a scheming noble-man attempts to influence the king to act against him. He alleges in Guillaume's absence that any attempt on the hero's part to conquer the pagan lands will result in defeat and the loss of the king's subjects. There is no sign that Louis accepts his judgment, but the incident is reported to Guillaume by Walter of Toulouse and Guillaume strides back into the assembly and, without further investigation, kills his detractor. The nobleman is Aymon and he is described as aged. There is no mention of any previous enmity between him and Guillaume, and the whole incident shows the hero-intruder at his most characteristic—violent, unthinking, and entirely concerned with his own reputation.

In all the epics of the Guillaume cycle, the hero is an intensely physical person, greedy in his appetites, terrible in his rages, uninhibited in his speech, and violent in his actions. It is hard to see why he is sometimes described as "prudent," since, even in his dealings with his king, he is often insulting, and his speeches are not in his own best interests.

The explanation is that his reputation is the only thing which really concerns him. He will not allow himself to be outclassed, still less dominated, by any other nobleman, and this desire for glory leads him into adventures of a highly exotic nature. His entry into Nîmes with a party of men concealed in barrels is reminiscent of the *Arabian Nights,* and his penetration of the Saracen palace at Orange disguised as a Turk has elements of farce. Yet each incident shows the typical features of the intrusion of the hero. Indeed, they are so accurately portrayed, even if in deliberately distorted form, that a suspicion of parody is justified.

Only in the Vivien epics does the tone become serious, and the theme of the intruder-hero is played down. The reason for this is at least partly that the Vivien epics are less homogeneous. They are not concentrated on a major event, as are the others, and there is some reason for believing that they are a conflation of different stories. In any event, the opposition between Christianity and paganism, as distinct from opposition between pagans and Christians, becomes far more important, as does the incompetence of Louis as a leader for Christianity. In the epics already discussed, Louis' weaknesses affect the internal conduct of his court, his inability to control his nobles, and the situation is not unlike that in the *Cid*. In the Vivien epics the situation is much more serious. It comes close to representing what might have happened in the *Chanson de Roland* if Charlemagne had not been brought to his senses.

Loyalty to kingship and its embodiments is unshakable in Guillaume. Even when Louis is at his feeblest, Guillaume sustains him and he not only makes no attempt to supplant him but deals firmly with any others who attempt to do so. Guillaume does, of course, become a territorial lord in his own right, like the Cid and Siegfried, but there is no question of his renouncing his loyalty to his sovereign.

The challenge to the king stops short of supplanting him, and this fact points to the reason why the Guillaume epics cannot be compared with the *Chanson de Roland* as social documents. The conflict between the hero and the king is seen entirely from the point of view of the hero. Its social implications are of little importance, although the results of the succession of a feeble monarch are made clear enough. The Guillaume epics are, indeed, the poems of the adventures of Guillaume. They use the conventions of "heroic" behavior in the face of the establishment to set up a series of rather repetitive tales, the adventures of an attractive fighting man, but they never produce true epic tension.

Poema del mio Cid, like *Beowulf* and the Oxford version of the *Chanson de Roland*, has come down to us in only one manuscript (made by Pedro Abbat in 1307 and preserved in the archives of Bivar, near Burgos, closely associated with the *Cid*), and even this manuscript lacks the opening lines.[22] Yet its hero, Ruy Díaz, appears in chronicles and many other literary forms and certainly

---

22. *Poema de Mio Cid,* Colin Smith, ed. (4th ed.; Oxford: Clarendon Press, 1972); Ramon Menendez Pidal, ed. (Madrid: B. Ballière, 1911).

is as memorable a figure for Spanish legendary history as are Roland for France and Arthur for England.

What distinguishes the Cid from these figures is the amount of knowledge which we have of him which can legitimately be called historical fact. Even if we reject those features of the "historical" accounts which appear to be derived from literary sources, there is still a great deal of information extant about his life, his military exploits, and his relationship to his sovereign. We are thus able to make comparisons between the events of the poem and those recorded in other works, in a way that is possible for no other major epic. Furthermore the extant form of the poem was almost certainly composed at a time so close to the events it portrays that there would be members of its audience who were witnesses to them or had heard of them from eyewitnesses. In other words, there was little time for the "facts" to undergo modification in the sense of epic convention, heroic creation, and adjustment to epic themes.

The poem is therefore of great interest to any study of the conflict between the hero and the king because it should, more than any other epic, reflect the first selections of themes and events by an epic composer and their organization into poetic form. It is therefore very significant that, in this poem, the conflict between the hero and the king is as marked as in any of the works already studied.

Although the beginning of the poem is missing, it undoubtedly told of the exile of the Cid by King Alfonso. The reason for this exile, so far as it can be determined from other sources,[23] is that he had come into conflict with Count García Ordóñez when the latter was helping the King of Granada in an expedition against the Moorish King of Seville, from whom the Cid was collecting tribute for his sovereign, Alfonso of León and Castille. The description is as chaotic as the circumstances and the relations between the parties. Moors and Christians are in opposition and alliance, and subjects of the same king are in conflict. The one fact that emerges is that there is intense rivalry between groups

23. See introduction to Smith ed. above, note 22.

at the court of Alfonso, and it is by no means certain that the King can control the rivalry. The resemblance to the events in the Guillaume cycle is clear. In the *Cid*, however, the rivalry is polarized and becomes the main theme of the epic. The poem, quite deliberately, begins with the Cid at the lowest point of his fortunes. His enemies are triumphant, and the king has banished him. He must leave the kingdom or die, and he has no money to pay the soldiers who alone can restore his fame and fortune. The opening is totally uncharacteristic of epic poetry. There is no crisis, no confrontation, merely a portrait of a noble man at a low point in his fortunes. There is no immediate conflict between hero and king, because the king has already made his decision to exile the Cid and has thus assured the triumph of the family of García Ordóñez. Yet the whole poem is an account of the way in which the Cid overcomes these obstacles and both recovers his honor and crushes his enemies.

The sentence of exile is, of course, passed by the king and, in that sense, the Cid and his sovereign are diametrically opposed. The Cid must overcome the king's opposition in order to return to the only society with which he is concerned, that of Castille and Léon. To do this he must operate outside its boundaries and ultimately induce the king to allow him to return. He is an exile from his own land, but, when he returns, it is as the lord of many lands outside Léon, as a foreign sovereign and potential rival.

His methods of rehabilitating himself are undoubtedly closer to the reality of warrior-experience than are those of any other epics. There are no dragons to overcome, no gods fighting for him or against him, no stylized battles. The Cid's encounters are of the real stuff of border warfare, with permissible exaggeration, and his objects are two—the acquisition of wealth and the reestablishment of reputation.

The rehabilitation follows a carefully organized pattern. The first essential is to secure money to pay soldiers and this is done by tricking money out of the Jews Raquel and Vidas. Even when the Cid has acquired vast wealth, this money is not repaid. The expeditions against Castejón and Alcocer are highly successful but they are no more than well-conducted minor operations for booty, easily distinguishable from epic contests. The battle against the Moorish force which follows is much closer to a conventional epic struggle, with its defeat of two Moorish kings, but the culminating point of these battles is not the slaughter but the distribution of spoil. Despoiling of armor is important in the *Iliad* and, as we have seen, disagreement over spoils has serious consequences in the poem, but I know of no Western epic in which so much attention is paid to spoils as in the *Cid*. There are several reasons for this. First, the poem is much closer to the reality of border warfare, where soldiers fought for shares in booty. Second, and from the literary point of view much more important, the Cid must use booty to resolve the conflict between himself and Alfonso. Like the majority of epic heroes, the Cid is concerned to keep the loyalty of his immediate dependents by speedy and generous division of spoils. By doing so, he ensures their loyalty and builds up an effective personal army through which he can exert power—and leverage on King Alfonso.

> . . . refechos son todos esos christianos con aquesta ganançia.
> A sos castiellos a los moros dentro los an tornados;
> mando mio Çid aun que les diessen algo.
> Grant a el gozo mio Çid con todos sos vassalos.
> Dio a partir estos dineros y estos averes largos,
> en la su quinta al Çid caen .c. cavallos;
> ¡Dios, que bien pago a todos sus vassalos. . . . (800–06)

(All the Christians are encouraged with this spoil. He brings the Moors back to their castles and orders that something should be given to them. The Cid shares the great joy of all his vassals. He has the money and the massive spoil shared out. A hundred horses fall to the Cid as part of his fifth. God, how well he pays all his vassals!)

Once he has satisfied his men, the Cid can turn his attention to the authorities. He donates money to the church under whose protection he has left his wife and daughters and sends a carefully judged present to the king. The thirty equipped chargers dispatched with Minaya Alvar Fañez constitute exactly the right kind of gift. It is large enough to be worthy of a monarch but not large enough to be a bribe. Alfonso's response is appropriate— he does not pardon the Cid, although he hints that he will do so, but he does pardon Minaya himself and, more important, he permits recruiting for the Cid's army. In doing so, he calls attention to the fact that those who have followed the Cid have put themselves outside the law and that the Cid's legal status is, to put it mildly, dubious. By this act Alfonso restores legality to the Cid's acts, even though those acts are carried on outside his jurisdiction. The king is attempting to make sure that his exiled subject does not slip from his grasp. In this he is aided by the Cid's extraordinary sense of loyalty to his sovereign, the same kind of loyalty which Guillaume gave to Louis. It would not be too much to say that Alfonso, now and later, is trading on this loyalty. There is at this point no reaction from the García family.

The Cid continues his depredations with an ever increasing army. We are told of three years of such expeditions, but the next turning point comes at the capture of Valencia. With the occupation of these lands the Cid becomes a landed proprietor, who rewards his followers with land as well as money and is thus no longer a raider but a ruler in his own right and who thus turns into a potential rival of Alfonso himself. The exile-hero has not intruded on the king's lands but he has used the king's subjects to establish himself as an independent monarch. The Cid is perfectly well aware of the legal and social situation. He sets up the most Draconic regulations to prevent his men from returning to León and Castille. He takes care, however, to safeguard his legal position by sending a much larger gift of one hundred equipped chargers to Alfonso and asks in exchange that his wife and daughters be allowed to join him. The portrait of the Cid is certainly that of a warm family man, but it should not be forgotten that the return of his wife and daughters would deprive the king of valuable potential hostages. It is particularly important for him to do this since he has taken it upon himself to set up a bishopric, definitely an act of a territorial prince.

En tierras de Valençia fer quiero obispado
e dar gelo a este buen christiano. (1299 f.)

("I want to set up a bishopric in the lands of Valencia and
to give it to this good Christian.")

Alfonso listens to the account of the Cid's deeds given by
Minaya and accepts the gifts. Before he has heard the Cid's re-
quests, Count García Ordóñez makes a sarcastic comment on the
Cid's deeds and is promptly silenced. The departure of the Cid's
ladies is granted and, further, all those who serve the Cid are
restored to favor. It will be noted that in doing this the king is
also restoring his authority over these men. He does not, at this
point, restore the Cid to his honors but the García family is overcome with foreboding. They follow the course, common in epic,
of trying to ingratiate themselves with the successful exile. The
Cid presents a real danger to them, particularly as he gives every
sign of regarding himself as the permanent lord of Valencia.

All the communications between the Cid and Alfonso have
been carried out in the same way—Minaya with an escort seeking
out the king and giving him presents and messages and thus performing that duty as intermediary which is essential to preserve
the honor of both sovereign and hero. His last journey of this sort
shows one or two interesting variations. He takes two hundred
equipped horses as a present, and indication of the magnitude of
the Cid's victories, but also two hundred of a mounted escort,
with instructions,

"que non diga mal el rey Alfonso del que Valençia manda."
(1814)

(Let King Alfonso speak no ill of him who rules in Valencia.)

The lesson is not lost on the king's court, the García family, or
the king himself. This group of "messengers" has the appearance—and the power—of an army and the announcement that
the Cid has inflicted a major defeat on Jusuf, King of Morocco,
is not likely to inspire confidence in a king who, so far as we are

told in the poem, never wins a single military victory. We have now reached the classic point of confrontation. The hero is in a position to challenge the king's authority, perhaps even to dethrone him, since he has a large trained military force which is utterly faithful to him. The king hastens to honor the leaders of the group and makes it very clear that he considers the Cid to be acting in his name. It is in conversation with the García family—apparently the cause of the Cid's exile—that he admits that he did wrong in banishing the Cid. Why does he now confess this? The original situation which brought about the exile has never been discussed, and the reason for Alfonso's change of heart is probably fear rather than penitence. When the García's propose that their sons marry the Cid's daughters, he is careful to give no decision but prefers to use the possibility as an excuse for pardoning the Cid and summoning him to court. He even leaves the place of meeting to the Cid, an act of generosity indeed but also an act of wisdom.

The Cid is pleased at the king's rehabilitation, but his reaction to it and the proposed marriages is couched in interesting terms:

"¡Esto gradesco a Christus el mio senor!
Echado fu de tierra e tollida la onor,
con grand afan gane lo que he yo;
a Dios lo gradesco que del rey he su [amor]
e piden me mis fijas pora los ifantes de Carrion.
Ellos son mucho urgullosos e an part en la cort,
deste casamiento no avria sabor;
mas pues lo conseja el que mas vale que nos
fablemos en ello, en la poridad seamos nos. (1933–41)

(Thanks be to Christ my Lord! I was driven from the land and my honor was taken from me. What I have now, I have won with great hardship. I thank God that I now have the king's love and that he asks my daughters of me for the princes of Carrión. They are of great position and highly placed at court. I have no taste for this marriage, but since he who advises it is of greater power than I, let us talk about it in secret.)

He links his return to grace with his own efforts and is definitely of the opinion that he has won his way back. He also feels that he had put the king in the position of having to ask for favors. The Cid's instincts tell him that he should beware of an alliance with a great noble family who must seek some advantage in offering marriage to someone of much lower social standing who is their enemy. It is clear even at this stage that he will accept the marriage only if the king himself accepts the responsibility.

It is interesting that it is the king who awaits the arrival of the Cid and not vice versa and although the Cid proffers his allegiance in due form, the king greets him as a virtual equal and is at some pains to be the first to provide entertainment. The marriage question is settled in terms which are utterly ambiguous. The king begs a favor—that the Cid will give his daughters in marriage to the princes. The Cid hedges—his daughters are too young, the Carrión princes of high estate—but he will obey the king in everything. Alfonso is thus forced into the position of making the decision. That decision includes dispatching the princes to Valencia, which seems to imply that Alfonso assumes that the Cid's domains are under his jurisdiction. However this may be, the Cid is careful to avoid the legal formality of handing over his daughters to the princes. He asks the king to hand them over through a deputy. These matters are of great importance for subsequent developments, for they place the king in a position of legal responsibility towards the Cid and against the Carrión family. Any future conflict is bound to pit Alfonso against one of two groups, the Cid family or the Carrión family, and the Cid is careful to ensure that, legally, the king is responsible for the marriage and its consequences and is therefore obliged to deal with any challenges which may result.

It may be well to sum up the position at this point. The king has asserted his authority first by his exile of the Cid for, apparently, acting against the interest of powerful subjects, the García (Carrión) family, but in doing so he has clearly not considered either his own true interests or those of his kingdom, since it is made clear throughout the poem that this family is utterly selfish and concerned only to manipulate the kingdom for personal gain. His forgiveness of the Cid is certainly motivated to a large degree, if not entirely, by the Cid's material gains. He naturally appreciates his prowess, but it is the tangible evidence, the chargers, the lands, and the formidable military force which the Cid can muster which bring about his change of heart.

The Carrión family despises the Cid. To them he is a dangerous upstart, a parvenu adventurer. They are depicted as degenerate aristocracy, whose only concern is to gain the maximum material advantage from their privileged position at court and from their obvious influence with the king. Their position is entirely parasitical. They contribute nothing to the welfare of Castille or León and would clearly not support Alfonso if it were against their interests. The failure of the king to see through their machinations in the early part of the poem indicates that he, like Charlemagne and Louis, is far from being an all-wise king. It requires violent action by the Cid to unmask them. The author makes it clear that his sympathies lie with the upward-striving elements of society represented by the Cid and that he expects rulers to favor them at the expense of an aristocratic establishment which has outlived its usefulness.

The decision by the author to begin his poem at the nadir of his hero's fortunes is clearly in accord with medieval concepts of ''comedy.'' He has lost the favor of his king, is about to be exiled, and is totally without material resources. He does, however, retain the affection and support of his wife, daughters, and a few faithful followers. His upward movement is that of any exile, and it is carried out independently of Alfonso. First he acquires money by trickery, then booty and hence more soldiers, and finally land and the prestige of a ruler. All this takes time— more than three years. At the end of it the Cid is a territorial prince but—and from the point of view of the epic, this is most important—he still regards himself as a subject of King Alfonso and is prepared to recognize him as his overlord. The poet stresses this loyalty, as might be expected, just as the author of *Beowulf* stresses the good faith of his hero both to Hrothgar and the family of Hygelac. But we cannot ignore the fact that the Cid can now call the tune and that he is prepared to cause Alfonso to act in his interests, first, in recognizing him and granting him formal pardon, and second, in taking responsibility for marriages for which the Cid would never have dared to ask himself. It should be remembered that these marriages would have redounded very much to the Cid's honor if the young princes of Carrión had been sensible enough to give at least lip service to their authenticity.

The events after the marriage constitute a series of confrontations, many of them legal, which demonstrate the conflict between the Cid, technically the outsider at Alfonso's court, and the family of Carrión, the insiders and representatives of the establishment. First, the physical cowardice of the Carrión princes is established in the lion incident (2278 ff.), which shows them as ignoble and the Cid and his men as generous. Their behavior in battle is equally embarrassing, and the poet has made his point: they are unworthy as nobles in the service of the king and still less worthy of being the Cid's sons-in-law.

What is not so clear is why, in the face of all this evidence, the Cid allows the arrangements for the marriage to continue, for it seems that it has not yet been solemnized, still less consummated. He does not investigate their highly suspicious behavior in the battle and allows them to receive a huge amount of booty. It is, apparently, their consciousness of wealth which makes them conceive their plot against his daughters. There is, of course, no reason why they should not take their wives to their lands in Carrión or why the Cid should not load them with honors and wealth. Yet we are told that he is suspicious, and he does send Félix Muñoz with them. It is very hard to escape the conclusion that he is more concerned about the preservation of the marriage than with his daughters' welfare. Just as surprising is the failure of the Moor Abengalbón to tell the Cid of the plot.

The poet is, of course, concerned to paint the princes of Carrión in as black colors as possible, and their beating of defenseless women condemns them utterly. Why then does Alfonso, who apparently hears of the event before the Cid does, not take action against them? It must be remembered that he bears the legal responsibility for the marriages. Yet we are told only that "he was grieved in his heart." The legal situation is quite complex. The women had passed into the tutelage of the princes, but those princes had now abandoned them and boasted that they were too low for their wedding couch, not fit even to be their concubines (2758 ff.). This is a direct insult to Alfonso, their feudal overlord, and action is called for. He takes none and thus proves what we have suspected throughout the poem, that he will act only when driven to it by more powerful wills.

The Cid's own reaction is typical if hardly humane. The "shameful thing" has been done to him and he will yet marry his daughters well. There is at no point any expression of sorrow either by him or his immediate followers at the *pain* the girls have suffered but only at their dishonor. This dishonor, one feels, is rather the Cid's than that of his daughters, and his "revenge" will consist, in part, in finding them better marriages.

> "¡Par aquesta barba   que nadi non messo
> non la lograran   los ifantes de Carrión,
> que a mis fijas   bien las casare yo!" (2832–34)

> (By this beard, which no one has ever touched, the princes of Carrión shall not succeed in preventing me from marrying my daughters well.)

From the point of view of our epic theme, the matter of chief concern is the action the Cid will take in respect of the king. He apologizes to his daughters that he had no choice but to accept the marriages, although it is far from clear from the earlier text that such was in fact the case. The remark is the first indication of the Cid's method of procedure. He is going to take the matter before the royal court on several grounds. The first and most important is that he has been dishonored in the treatment of his daughters and that he has been deprived of material goods, those, presumably, which he gave to the princes of Carrión in the belief that they were honest sons-in-law. Such a proceeding is common in medieval lawsuits. What is not so common is the Cid's statement that the king has been more dishonored than he has himself. This means, of course, that the king is not merely a judge in a quarrel between two of his subjects but that he is being forced by the Cid into a position of having to oppose the García family.

> "Lieves el mandado   a Castiella al rey Alfonsso;
> por mi besa le la mano   d'alma e de coraçon
> —cuemo yo so su vassallo   y el es mio señor—
> desta desondra que me an fecha   los ifantes de Carrión
> quel pese al buen rey   d'alma e de coraçon.
> El caso mis fijas,   ca non gelas di yo;
> quando las han dexadas   a grant desonor
> si desondra i cabe   alguna contra nos
> la poca e la grant   toda es de mio senor. (2903–11)

(Take this message to Castille, to King Alfonso. Kiss his hand for me from my soul and heart, for I am his vassal and he my lord. Let the good king weigh in soul and heart this disgrace which the princes of Carrión have put on me. The marriage of my daughters did not come from me. Since they have been cast off with great dishonor, some disgrace falls on us from this, but great or small, it all falls on my lord.)

The king does indeed summon a court, after admitting his responsibility and brushes aside the García request to be excused from attending.

It is very important to note the parallel here to the trial of Ganelon in the *Chanson de Roland*. There, too, it was the king and his policy which were actually on trial. Had he the right to crush private vengeance in the name of public policy? And should he not have used his powers as sovereign to prevent the situation from arising at all? The second point is certainly as applicable to Alfonso as it was to Charlemagne, for his weakness in being swayed to exile the Cid and then failing to see through the schemes of the García family or to punish them when those schemes were put into action is the true cause of the trial. The king is really on trial himself and the Cid is thus in the position of having to prove that Alfonso must be obeyed rather than of defending his own honor.

It is worth noting that the Cid arrives (late) in the manner of an independent ruler. He wisely refuses to sit with Alfonso on the judgment seat (3114 f.). The king's opening remarks seem to prejudge the matter, but the Cid, in his statement to the judges, is again at pains to point out that it is the king's honor which is at stake.

> "por mis fijas quem dexaron   yo non he desonor,
> ca vos las casastes, rey,   sabredes que fer oy;" (3149 f.)

> (I am not dishonored because of my daughters whom they cast off, my king, for it is you who gave them in marriage and you know what is to be done today.)

He obtains his swords and his material goods from the princes of Carrión by giving the impression that he will not press the matter of his daughters. Only when he has them does he turn to the matter of the breaking of the marriages. Here the real conflict comes into the open. The García-Carrión group maintain that there can be no question of dishonor because their own rank is so far above that of the Cid's family that they were right, legally and morally, to reject the Cid's daughters, the offspring of a mere knight. The point is not so ridiculous as it seems. Neither the Garcías nor the Cid would have regarded a peasant as having any honor to be avenged. The matter is in the hands of the judges and, in the last instance, in those of the king. He decides in favor of the Cid and calls on the Carrión family to appear in three weeks to defend themselves against three of the Cid's champions.

If the king had not been involved, if the Cid had not emphasized the question of honor, and still more if the Cid had not been a ruler of tremendous resources, it is improbable that he would have decided in this way. The exile, the upstart, has succeeded. The confrontation in this epic takes the form of an intruder into society, an upward-striver whose determination to rise causes him to fall foul of the establishment at Alfonso's court. They have enough power to make a weak, if good-natured king drive the Cid into exile. The story is concerned with this exile's acquisition of the means to reverse this decision, first by gradually influencing the king to reverse his legal disabilities, then by getting himself recognized as a powerful landed vassal, not a mere adventurer knight. The marriages with the princes of Carrión seem to indicate that his penetration of the court establishment has succeeded, especially since he insists that the king arrange the marriages. The breakdown of the arrangement proves the king's lack of control over his powerful subjects, the García family; and the necessity of an alliance with the Cid in order to crush them. This second effort, brought about by legal means but with obvious partisanship on the part of Alfonso, ruins the family and shatters their power. Henceforth there will be an alliance between León, Castille, and Valencia, an alliance fortified by the new marriages of the Cid's daughters. A new order has thus been created. The king remains, his rule apparently intact, but his throne rests on the support of very different men, men who will be restless and adventurous, not passive and greedy.

It was pointed out at the beginning of this study of the Cid that it begins, as a medieval "comedy" should, with its hero at the nadir of his fortunes and his enemies apparently triumphant. The ending also is that of a comedy. The Cid is totally triumphant, his daughters do indeed make the better marriages he promised them. The judicial combat which ostensibly decides the case brought by the Cid is a predictable farce, with total victory for the Cid's champions. The future for the Cid looks very bright indeed. Any reader of epics will realize that this is a highly unusual state of affairs. Epics frequently end in tragedy for their major figures—Roland, Beowulf, Siegfried, Gunther, Hagen—and even if they survive, as do Agamemnon, Achilles, Aeneas, Charlemagne, and Guillaume, they suffer great personal loss and their prospects are gloomy. Even the *Odyssey* can hardly be said to end cheerfully. Furthermore, there is always a question of the stability of epic society. In some works, notably the *Nibelungenlied*, it is shattered. In *Beowulf* survival is doubtful at best, and there are deep forbodings in the *Iliad* and the Charlemagne epics. The *Aeneid* looks forward to a new society but at great cost to those already established. Only in the *Cid* can we say that society takes on new life. Its hero is not faced with a powerful force of evil but a socially inimical group. His fight for fame and fortune is not directed against his sovereign nor does he think in terms of a confrontation with him. His actions expose his king's weakness and indecision, as do those of Beowulf, Roland, and Guillaume, but they do not bring about his fall. The Cid wishes to enter into the old society, not shatter it or even reshape it. The king is shrewd enough to see where his own interests lie and to adjust his policy accordingly. Only the degenerate aristocratic establishment suffers.

This pragmatism is almost certainly due to the chronological proximity of the epic to the events it describes. Its challenges and confrontations are those of the history of the Spanish border, not those of developed epic. Nevertheless the clash between the hero, in his pursuit of power, and his king is clear enough. It is interesting to speculate what would have happened if the king had not been wise enough to forgive the Cid and to support him in his struggle with the García-Carrión family.

The study of the *Odyssey* has deliberately been postponed to the end. It is the exile work of all exile works, and it may well be asked how there can be in this epic any struggle between a hero and a king in the sense in which the theme has been discussed in relation to earlier epics. The kings who actually appear in the story are on its fringes—Menelaus and Nestor, visited by Telemachus, and numerous kings in Hades. The only major regal figure is Alcinous, of whom more will be said. Odysseus never comes into conflict with any of these figures. Even in the numerous raids of which he tells in his long account of his wanderings he does not meet or confront anyone who could be called a king in the way the term has been used of Agamemnon, Charlemagne, Hrothgar, or Gunther. On the other hand, Odysseus is himself a king in the Homeric sense. He rules a land, he has subjects, he dispenses justice. When Eumaeus the swineherd is describing his master to Odysseus in his beggar's clothes, he talks at great length of his power and possessions. Ithaca was not Mycenae or Troy, and Odysseus himself has no illusions about its greatness, but it is a kingdom, large enough and prosperous enough to support its inhabitants in comfort (IX, 25–28).

For almost all the poem, however, Odysseus is not in the position of a king and only rarely does he achieve any recognition of his status and rank. What is more important still is that his palace is occupied by suitors, men of his own and neighboring islands, who hope to win his wife Penelope and in doing so to deprive Telemachus of his birthright. These suitors are noblemen but they are not kings. The situation as the poem opens is thus very different from that which we find in most epics—and deliberately so. For in the *Iliad*, the *Chanson de Roland*, the *Cid*, and the *Nibelungenlied* we are shown almost at once a confrontation between a recognized ruler and an intruder who is intent on his own interests. Only in *Beowulf* is the opening anything like that in the *Odyssey*, and in very significant respects. At both courts there is chaos because of the impact of evil outsiders and the inability of established authority to deal with them. At Heorot the evil was not human and was bent only on the destruction of a center of religion and civilization, and its success was largely due, as we have seen, to the weakness of an aging king. This is not so in the *Odyssey*. It is made very clear that the situation there is due to one thing—the aftermath of the Trojan War. The suitors are in the hall of Odysseus because they *believe* him to be dead—but they do not know. Penelope stalls and refuses to make a decision because she *hopes* that Odysseus is still alive—but she does not know. The early books are filled with parallel accounts of those who returned and ruled—Nestor and Menelaus—and those who returned and died—Agamemnon. The fate of Odysseus remains poised. Many have heard of him at various stages in his long homecoming, but none knows now where he is. The world of Ithaca is still suspended in the state it was nineteen years before. It is awaiting the return of its ruler and hence of authority. Until that authority returns, that world will be turned upside down, waiting for a woman's decision and suffering from the depredations of selfish intruders. Even Telemachus, now grown to manhood, cannot act independently, since the property in which he lives does not belong to him.

The palace at Ithaca is like Heorot in being occupied by evil but, in accordance with the general plan of the *Odyssey*, not by overwhelming or universal evil but rather by antisocial forces of no great stature or frightening aspect. The wickedness consists in improvidence, misuse of another man's property, and coveting his wife. We rarely see the suitors do anything but eat, drink, play, and listen to stories (I, 421 ff.). Theirs is very definitely a peacetime, unheroic existence. Their life is a product of a masterless realm, and everyone, down to the lowest servant, is aware of this. Each hopes for an early solution—although not the same one—for to all the prevailing chaos is appalling. The poem opens with the beginnings of that solution.

The council on Olympus is significant, not least because of the fact that it begins the poem. The fate of Odysseus has become a cosmic matter. Zeus recalls several other homecomings from Troy and the horrors associated with them, and it is Athena who reminds him that the fate of Odysseus, against whom no wrongdoing can be urged, still remains unresolved. In fact, only Poseidon is against him—and he is away from Olympus. The role of supernatural power is thus established. Zeus will be benevolently neutral and will permit the Odysseus situation to move off center. Poseidon will play the role of spoiler, but his influence is confined to making things difficult at sea. He cannot prevent Odysseus' movement home. The positive force comes from Athena. She is no longer the angry goddess rejected by Paris but the constructive civilizing force of social life. Her battle role appears only at the slaughter of the suitors. Otherwise she is concerned to use wisdom and cunning, lies and disguises to achieve her ends. In this Odysseus is her pupil, although at times he seems to be ahead of her thinking. In other words, we are going to be presented with an epic of civil virtue, of sense and thought, not braggart behavior or defiance. The exile must return home again.

There is thus no confrontation between an intruding, self-centered hero and a settled ruler nor, on the surface, are great issues involved. Yet the essential theme is as clear as ever. In this world-to-be-restored, the position of the ruler is usurped by self-centered intruders, and the role of intruder-hero is played by the king. We shall discuss the clash in some detail.

It has been remarked that the opening of the poem is at a point of suspense. The same is true of Odysseus himself. He has been on the island of Ogygia for seven years, and at this point his exile appears to be unending. He is held not by hostile forces, but by a woman with divine powers who has taken him in from the sea and who loves him. The conflict in his mind is thus between a perfectly pleasant life of ease and a yearning for his island home and his wife Penelope.

«Διογενὲς Λαερτιάδη, πολυμήχαν᾽ Ὀδυσσεῦ,
οὕτω δὴ οἶκόνδε φίλην ἐς πατρίδα γαῖαν
αὐτίκα νῦν ἐθέλεις ἰέναι; σὺ δὲ χαῖρε καὶ ἔμπης.
εἴ γε μὲν εἰδείης σῇσι φρεσὶν ὅσσα τοι αἶσα
κήδε᾽ ἀναπλῆσαι, πρὶν πατρίδα γαῖαν ἱκέσθαι,
ἐνθάδε κ᾽ αὖθι μένων σὺν ἐμοὶ τόδε δῶμα φυλάσσοις
ἀθάνατός τ᾽ εἴης, ἱμειρόμενός περ ἰδέσθαι
σὴν ἄλοχον, τῆς αἰὲν ἐέλδεαι ἤματα πάντα.
οὐ μέν θην κείνης γε χερείων εὔχομαι εἶναι,
οὐ δέμας οὐδὲ φυήν, ἐπεὶ οὔ πως οὐδὲ ἔοικε
θνητὰς ἀθανάτῃσι δέμας καὶ εἶδος ἐρίζειν.»
Τὴν δ᾽ ἀπαμειβόμενος προσέφη πολύμητις Ὀδυσσεύς·
«πότνα θεά, μή μοι τόδε χώεο· οἶδα καὶ αὐτὸς
πάντα μάλ᾽, οὕνεκα σεῖο περίφρων Πηνελόπεια
εἶδος ἀκιδνοτέρη μέγεθός τ᾽ εἰσάντα ἰδέσθαι·
ἣ μὲν γὰρ βροτός ἐστι, σὺ δ᾽ ἀθάνατος καὶ ἀγήρως.
                                        V, 203-18[24]

("So, my clever Odysseus, divinely descended son of Laertes, you really do wish to start for home at once, to the dear land

24. *Homeri opera*, Thomas W. Allen, ed. Vols. 3 and 4: *Odyssey* (2d ed.; Oxford: Clarendon Press, 1919).

of your fathers. Good luck go with you! But if you had the least idea what miseries you are to suffer before you reach your native soil, you would stay here with me, keep to this house, and become immortal, even though you never stop wishing to see that wife of yours and brood about her every day. Yet I protest that I am no worse than she in face and figure. It is not right that a mortal should contend with a goddess in looks and appearance.'' Then Odysseus of the nimble wits replied and said: "Lady goddess, do not be annoyed with me about this. I am well aware myself that wise Penelope is altogether inferior to you in looks and stature. After all, she is a mortal and you are a goddess and ageless.'')

The female element is significant. Odysseus himself says (at least to Calypso herself) that she is infinitely more beautiful than his wife Penelope. She presumably has the advantage also that, as a goddess, she does not age. It is not as a female, even as a lover, that Odysseus yearns for Penelope but as a symbol of hearth and home. Throughout the work he has various sexual liaisons. None of them has the slightest relation to his feeling about his home, of which Penelope is an essential, perhaps the essential, part. It is women much more than men who influence his actions and decide his fate. His courage and, more often, his cunning can usually deal with men. He is often rash, as he is with the Cyclops, and he and even more his men pay the penalty of his desire to outwit his opponents. Many of his acts are, in fact, the typical "exile-raid,'' the very thing which Hrothgar's coast warden feared and in which Hygelac died.

But in this poem they are not turning points in the hero's fortunes. The force that comes closest to destroying him is the sea and its god Poseidon, the hostile element which divides from home, which is unproductive and makes a man into an exile. It is the conquest of the power of the sea which occupies much of the poem and provides much of the adventure in the epic, but this conquest is incidental to the main theme—the restitution of society by the exiled king.

The crucial acts of rescue, the decisions which save Odysseus from the powers which are holding him back from his home, are performed by females. It is Circe who instructs him to go on the voyage to the dead, where he learns the fate that awaits him and where he compares himself with the other heroes who left Troy or who were left there. His troubles are by no means ended when he returns from the dead, but his future is assured. As Circe says, he has died one death, enough for most men (XII, 21 ff.). It is Circe who directs him on the road home. Again the power of the sea shatters his ship, his crew is lost, and he is thrown on the mercies of Calypso on the isle of Ogygia.

Only when she is ordered by the gods does Calypso let him go; she has held him not because she hates him but because she wants him for her own. It is the situation we find frequently in romance, the lady who forgets her social obligations in her desire for possession. As a goddess, Calypso can be informed of her selfishness only by the king of the gods. She is resentful but not so much so that she fails to provide Odysseus with the means to sail to his homeland, even as she tells him of his foolishness in leaving a life of ease with her for the hardships of the voyage. She too has to yield to the need for society to be reconstructed. Again Poseidon's sea shatters Odysseus' vessel and again it is a female, this time the sea nymph Leucothoe, who saves him, motivated by pity (V, 339 ff.). The scene is, indeed, a picture of conflict between the sea, stirred by Poseidon, and Athena and the power of Leucothoe's veil. It is the female powers which triumph, and Odysseus is safely on shore in Phaeacia.

The Alcinous episode is worth detailed study. Odysseus has landed not as a powerful exile-intruder but as a naked and totally destitute outcast. His reception follows the familiar pattern, but its features are remodeled in accordance with the nonmilitary, peacetime-society basis of the whole poem. When Odysseus presents himself, it is not to a coast warden or a group of warriors but to the king's daughter, engaged, somewhat lightheartedly, in washing the family linen. Her occupation does not prevent her from behaving with courage worthy of her heritage. It is she who takes over the function of the nobleman who guides the intruder to the palace, pointing him as usual along the highroad, even if it is a disguised Athena who finally leads him there.

The palace, as it is described, is as far from a military fortress as can be imagined. Our attention is called to it through the gaze of Odysseus, who sees here the very perfection of social life, the ideal to which he is attempting to return and which he is determined to restore. Odysseus does not approach as a blustering hero. There is no question of the stacking of arms or of challenges. He does not go to Alcinous the king but, as he has been instructed, to Arete, the queen (VII, 146 ff.). It is never made clear why he should approach her, since this is not an overtly matriarchal government, and it is Alcinous who makes the decisions. Nevertheless the technique of appealing as a suppliant to the queen is successful. His success may be due in part to the unusual nature of his plea, for instead of asking to be received as a suppliant, in other words to be given at least a temporary home, he asks to be taken back to his homeland.

There is no other epic, to my knowledge, in which the hero asks to leave the court he has just entered. Furthermore, Odysseus does not say where that homeland is—nor does he state his identity. The question of the identity of the intruder-hero is always important, and the character attributed to him at this first encounter can affect the whole work, as it does in the *Nibelungenlied*. Yet Odysseus is not asked for his name until the evening after the games. His host has already agreed to give him passage home by this time (VII, 317 ff.).

Yet the question of identity is never far from the poet's mind— Demodocus the minstrel sings of Troy at the first evening meal and Alcinous notes Odysseus' distress. As Hagen told the exploits of Siegfried without knowing who he was and so established a myth which controlled later action, so the identity of Odysseus begins to control the actions of the Phaeacians. They realize that they are dealing with an unusual person, and his greatness is confirmed at the games. It will be observed that it is at the games that Odysseus encounters the envious critic who is an obligatory part of the reception of the intruder-hero. This is not the sharp challenge to Siegfried or the denigrating criticism of Unferth. It is merely an implication that Odysseus is over the hill so far as

games are concerned and even stronger implication that he was
never an athlete anyway. These are very obviously the actions
of a green adolescent who knows no better and who later tries
to make up for his bad manners. For it is no more than bad
manners. This is not an epic situation. It is an amusement for
men unused to real combat, in a gentle peacetime situation, and
it can be settled without any harm to anyone.

The establishing of Odysseus' identity continues through the
minstrel's songs. The song of the love-escapade of Ares and
Aphrodite, again an utterly unepic story suited to this unwarlike
society, is followed by the story of the fall of Troy, in which
Odysseus is described as a major actor. To the Phaeacians this
is their closest approach to war. For Odysseus, it is grim reality,
and at this point he yields to Alcinous' request to reveal his name.

σοὶ δ᾽ ἐμὰ κήδεα θυμὸς ἐπετράπετο στονόεντα
εἴρεσθ᾽, ὄφρ᾽ ἔτι μᾶλλον ὀδυρόμενος στεναχίζω·
τί πρῶτόν τοι ἔπειτα, τί δ᾽ ὑστάτιον καταλέξω;
κήδε᾽ ἐπεί μοι πολλὰ δόσαν θεοὶ οὐρανίωνες.
νῦν δ᾽ ὄνομα πρῶτον μυθήσομαι, ὄφρα καὶ ὑμεῖς
εἴδετ᾽, ἐγὼ δ᾽ ἂν ἔπειτα φυγὼν ὕπο νηλεὲς ἦμαρ
ὑμῖν ξεῖνος ἔω καὶ ἀπόπροθι δώματα ναίων.
εἴμ᾽ Ὀδυσεὺς Λαερτιάδης, ὅς πᾶσι δόλοισιν
ἀνθρώποισι μέλω, καί μευ κλέος οὐρανὸν ἵκει.   IX, 12-20

("Your mind is set on asking me about the wretched miseries
I suffer, so that I shall grieve even more in my sorrow. What
shall I tell first and last and in between? The gods in heaven
have sent me so many misfortunes. I shall first tell you my
name, so that you may know me and so that if I escape the
dread fates, I may be a guest-friend of yours, however far
from here I may dwell. I am Odysseus, son of Laertes, who
am known to all for my cleverness, and my fame has reached
the heavens.)

Suddenly the Phaeacians are involved and a man who has ex-
perienced war is among them and tells of events, not as a minstrel
but as an actor. For a little time they are themselves taking part
and some of them, the crew which ultimately took Odysseus to

Ithaca, suffer for their participation. Their sheltered existence for a time is affected by the real world, and so shattering is the experience that they change their way of life. Thus the destitute exile does, though not of his own volition, deeply affect the society he so briefly intrudes upon. His myth is too big for this rather self-satisfied society, kind and hospitable indeed but unsteeled to disaster—something they know of only from bards.

We should mention two other minor features of Odysseus' intrusion. The nobleman-intermediary who finds out the identity and purpose of the hero-intruder is here, and his function is to recall the king to his duty to help a suppliant. There is no need for fear, only the need to behave in civilized fashion. The role of Nausikaa has already been mentioned. She is the link between the recently landed stranger and the royal power. She is also potentially a means of keeping Odysseus at Phaeacia, as would be normal for an intruder-hero in an epic. She admires Odysseus (VIII, 457 ff.) and thinks of him in terms of marriage (VI, 244 f.). Her father says openly that he would be delighted to have him as a son-in-law.

τοῖος ἐὼν οἷός ἐσσι, τά τε φρονέων ἅ τ' ἐγώ περ,
παῖδά τ' ἐμὴν ἐχέμεν καὶ ἐμὸς γαμβρὸς καλέεσθαι
αὖθι μένων· οἶκον δέ κ' ἐγὼ καὶ κτήματα δοίην,
εἴ κ' ἐθέλων γε μένοις·   VII, 312-15

("You are a man who thinks as I do and I wish you would take my child, stay here, and be called my son-in-law. I would give you a house and wealth—if you wanted to stay.")

Again Odysseus comes close to being tied to a woman at one of his landing points and to living a life of ease, and again it is his drive away from his point of intrusion towards his home which prevents it. It will be noted that this time Odysseus is not concerned with a goddess or a nymph. Nausikaa is the outstandingly beautiful daughter of a rich and powerful ruler. Odysseus could quite well have told one of the tales which he fabricates so easily and have married her. The point is that he may make up a new identity for himself for tactical reasons but throughout he remains true to his identity and to his purpose. He frequently causes trouble and disruption, and in this he is the characteristic exile-intruder, but there is no instance of the fall of an established ruler through his actions. His behavior resembles that of the hero in one respect only: he is bent on his return home and he has the single-mindedness to concentrate on his own fate.

The arrival in Ithaca ends the series of intrusions on other courts and other cultures. The question now is how Odysseus should tackle the problem. Although he is the rightful king, he has no power. *He* is the exile, and the power is in the hands of the suitors. His wife is a virtual prisoner, his father lives as a peasant, and only a few of his former household are faithful to his memory. In other words, the establishment is upside down. It is characteristic that he works out with Athena the best method of approach (XIII, 372 ff.). It is one of guile, not force, and it is pragmatic. Odysseus will go to the court as a beggar, bide his time, and wait for an opportunity. It will be remembered that Athena had made him look younger and more handsome at the court of Alcinous. Now he is made to look old and decrepit. The role he assumes is exactly the opposite of that of the hero-intruder. He approaches the hall as the lowest person in the social order and behaves towards the suitors with a humility he certainly does not feel.

His entry is via the swineherd's hut. It is here that his background story is told, not by an observant nobleman, and those acts in which a hero is usually entertained by a ruler are performed under the most sordid conditions. The swineherd is, in fact, a noble man, but the entry of this hero is a conscious reversal of epic tradition. The first revelation of identity also inverts tradition. There is no questioning by coast-wardens or noblemen. In a humble setting a father reveals himself to his—at first skeptical—son. It is not a great hero that Telemachus embraces but an ugly old man in rags. It says much for the young man that he accepts reality and welcomes his father. Telemachus is, after all, the nominal ruler of Odysseus' hall until the return of his father, but, as we have seen, the real rulers are the intruding suitors. The plan worked out between Odysseus and Telemachus is thus an attempt to destroy the intruders. The exile associates himself with the "ruler" against the intruders who actually rule. The hero-intruder does not stack his arms. He arranges to have the arms normally kept in the hall taken away. It is the intruder-suitors occupying the palace who lose their weapons, and the act is carried out by the hero and the titular ruler (xix, 1 ff.).

The incidents leading up to the destruction of the suitors must be explored in detail. Odysseus enters the hall limping and in rags. He receives food from Telemachus, and his first encounter with the suitors is a begging round in the course of which he is abused by Antinous (xvii, 445 ff.). The act is almost a parody of the conflict between the intruder-hero and the envious critic. The difference lies in the fact that there is no reconciliation.

Antinous is the first to die. He, alone of the suitors, actually strikes Odysseus as he makes his rounds and thus commits the offense of insulting the king—whom he naturally does not recognize. Much worse, however, he offends against the laws of hospitality, as his own cronies are quick to point out. Odysseus rebukes him as if he were indeed a king and on unusual grounds—that Antinous' brains are not commensurate with his birth or appearance (xvii, 453 ff.). Thus Odysseus' first appearance in the hall is a challenge, but it is a challenge to the suitors' sense of propriety, not of their valor. Antinous fails the test and in doing so behaves like an insolent brat. The audience is happy to see him suffer.

The parody of the heroic intrusion continues in the struggle between Odysseus and Iris. Again there is the mockery of the hero, the boasting and the reckoning, the blow that crushes Iris (xviii, 90 ff.). The clash of beggars parallels and hides the true nature of the clash which is taking place. The reckoning with the suitors is postponed by Odysseus' interview with Penelope. The parallels with his encounters with Circe, Calypso, Nausikaa, and Arete are obvious. What is important to notice is that Odysseus gives to Penelope the kind of information which is usually demanded by the ruler of the intruder or provided as a "hero-myth" by an informed nobleman.

Κρήτη τις γαῖ᾽ ἔστι, μέσῳ ἐνὶ οἴνοπι πόντῳ,
καλὴ καὶ πίειρα, περίρρυτος· ἐν δ᾽ ἄνθρωποι
πολλοί, ἀπειρέσιοι, καὶ ἐννήκοντα πόληες·
ἄλλη δ᾽ ἄλλων γλῶσσα μεμιγμένη· ἐν μὲν Ἀχαιοί,
ἐν δ᾽ Ἐτεόκρητες μεγαλήτορες, ἐν δὲ Κύδωνες,
Δωριέες τε τριχάϊκες δῖοί τε Πελασγοί·
τῇσι δ᾽ ἐνὶ Κνωσός, μεγάλη πόλις, ἔνθα τε Μίνως
ἐννέωρος βασίλευε Διὸς μεγάλου ὀαριστής,
πατρὸς ἐμοῖο πατήρ, μεγαθύμου Δευκαλίωνος.
Δευκαλίων δ᾽ ἐμὲ τίκτε καὶ Ἰδομενῆα ἄνακτα·
ἀλλ᾽ ὁ μὲν ἐν νήεσσι κορωνίσιν Ἴλιον εἴσω
οἴχεθ᾽ ἅμ᾽ Ἀτρεΐδῃσιν, ἐμοὶ δ᾽ ὄνομα κλυτὸν Αἴθων,
ὁπλότερος γενεῇ· ὁ δ᾽ ἄρα πρότερος καὶ ἀρείων. XIX, 172-84

(There is a land called Crete in the midst of the dark blue sea, beautiful and rich, surrounded by the waves. There are many people there, countless indeed, and ninety cities. Their speech is mixed, each group with its own. Among them are the Achaeans, the native Cretans, proud of heart, the Cydones, the Dorians with their three tribes, and the noble Pelasgians. Among the towns is Gnossos, a great city, and there Minos ruled nine years, a friend of almighty Zeus. He was the father of my father, the noble Deucalion. Deucalion begot me and Prince Idomeneus. But Idomeneus set out for Troy in his beaked ships with the sons of Atreus. I am the younger son, called Aethon, but he was the older and better.)

She makes a startling appearance in front of the suitors before she sees Odysseus and cleverly prevails on them to bring gifts (XVIII, 275 ff.). Odysseus admires her and here, as at other points, it seems almost that she knows who the beggar is, and is playing both with him and the suitors. The meeting between Penelope and the beggar takes place after the feast is over and the hall is quiet. Penelope tells the truth of her longing for Odysseus and of the havoc which his absence has brought about. Her statement is, in fact, the counterpart to the story of Odysseus himself. It is countered by his tale, true though told from a different point of view, of Odysseus' movements (XIX, 124 ff.). Again we have the myth of the hero which is as powerful as the hero himself. The presence of Odysseus grows ever stronger until it finally breaks into the open as Eurycleia recognizes the scar (XIX, 466 ff.). The beggar has finally been tied to the Odysseus of the past by an old woman who remembers. For this, surely, is the point of the scene, to bring the past and the present together, to combine the myth of Odysseus with the beggar physically present in the hall. It is immediately after this that Penelope tells her dream of the death of her suitors and that she proposes, with the agreement of Odysseus, to set up the trial of the bow. The decision seems astonishing after all her years of putting off the claimants. It could be explained as weariness of hope deferred too long, but within the terms of the epic it means that Penelope too senses the culmination, the man and the myth coming together and the test of the intruders by the king. And once again it is a woman who sets that test (XXI, 68 ff.).

It is easily said that the test of the bow is a typical example of the epic feature which sets tests for the hero. The winning of a bride by passing tests is common in fairy tales and the obvious parallel in the epics is the winning of Brunhilde, either by tests set by the gods or by the lady herself. The circumstances in the *Odyssey*, however, are very different. The purpose of the bow-test is to see whether any of the intruder-suitors can match Odysseus. In other words, Penelope is going to compare the strength of those who now seek her hand in marriage with that of her former husband and she is going to use an instrument, her husband's bow, to make that test.

It will be noted that the test is strictly a game. There is no question of one suitor's being more brave than another. There is no actual contest between warriors. The test is one of strength in stringing the bow and of skill in shooting an arrow straight. In this respect the test is much closer to the tournaments of medieval romance than to epic confrontations. Furthermore, the bow is not normally a heroic weapon. It will be recalled that Pandarus broke the truce between the Greeks and Trojans by his use of the bow, that it was a bow which, in late classical stories, brought about the death of Achilles, and that Waltharius has to dispose of a "treacherous" archer. It is typical of Odysseus that he is an expert with the bow, a weapon requiring more skill than strength, and that he should have devised the test, which Penelope so well remembers, in order to demonstrate that skill. Once again the suitors are being called upon to compete with the myth of Odysseus as it exists in the minds of his household. It is Telemachus— who already knows of Odysseus' identity—who sets up the axes in their trench and comes nearest to stringing the bow. All the others fail and Antinous, wisely, finds an excuse for postponing his own trial (xxi, 256 ff.). All the action takes place in the course of wine drinking and feasting and is simply part of a game.

Only when Odysseus the beggar asks to try the bow does a confrontation ensue. Antinous pronounces his own fate by citing the parallel of the Centaurs at the Lapith wedding banquet (xxi, 295 ff.), and again it is a woman, Penelope, who makes the decisive move. For she urges that Odysseus be given his chance— again as if she knew who he was—and it soon becomes apparent that it is the reflection on their reputation which is worrying the suitors. In the end, however, it is Telemachus who asserts his authority and ensures that Odysseus takes the bow. He looses the arrow and does not miss. The man has overtaken the myth and from now on there are no more games. Odysseus himself makes this clear:

Αὐτὰρ ὁ γυμνώθη ῥακέων πολύμητις Ὀδυσσεύς,
ἆλτο δ' ἐπὶ μέγαν οὐδόν, ἔχων βιὸν ἠδὲ φαρέτρην
ἰῶν ἐμπλείην, ταχέας δ' ἐκχεύατ' ὀϊστοὺς
αὐτοῦ πρόσθε ποδῶν, μετὰ δὲ μνηστῆρσιν ἔειπεν·
«οὗτος μὲν δὴ ἄεθλος ἀάατος ἐκτετέλεσται·
νῦν αὖτε σκοπὸν ἄλλον, ὃν οὔ πώ τις βάλεν ἀνήρ,
εἴσομαι, αἴ κε τύχωμι, πόρῃ δέ μοι εὖχος Ἀπόλλων.»

XXII, 1ff

(But Odysseus of the nimble wits stripped off his rags and sprang on to the great threshold with his bow and full quiver. He poured out the swift arrows in front of his feet and then spoke to the suitors: "This dread game is at an end. Now I shall aim at another target at which no man yet has ever shot. May Apollo grant my prayer that I strike home.")

From now on it is the intruder-hero who is really the king vindicating his rights against the temporary rulers of his hall. His destruction of them with the bow is deliberately shown as the slaughter of men like cattle. The suitors are not heroes to be faced in battle. They are people who have used the period of chaos after a war and the overlong absence of a master to disrupt civilized life. They are removed by that master so that civilized life may be restored. Although there is a final battle between Odysseus and his companions and the suitors who survive the arrows, its result is a foregone conclusion. It is a battle characterized by the simile which compares the dead suitors with piles of fish on the beach (XXII, 383 ff.). The ruler has cleansed his palace. He puts to death those women whom he regards as having defiled it by their conduct. All that remains is to prove to Penelope that he is indeed the Odysseus who left Ithaca so long ago and who has now returned to claim his own again. The last act of the story, as might be expected, is the winning again of the woman who represents the stability and continuity of civilized life.

The theme of the hero and the king is thus as strong in the *Odyssey* as in any of the epics, but it is inverted, and with good reason. The *Odyssey* is a work of restoration. It does not deal with the intruder-hero or the stranger who, under the impulse of social change or border warfare moves into an established kingdom and challenges it. Nor does it deal with the clash between the responsibilities of ruler and individual. In these clashes there is a challenge to established order and never does that order survive the hero's challenge unchanged. Only too often it is made clear that the ruler, or his system, or both, are irretrievably damaged and that a new order or chaos will soon ensue. The *Odyssey* deals with no such problem. The *Iliad* had already shown the challenge to the king and the devastating effect of irresponsibility, both public and private. The poem forecasts the collapse of Troy and the end of a civilization.

In the early books of the *Odyssey* we find that the war had left its scars on the victors too, and that they were changed. The purpose of the poem is to show that order can be reestablished and civilization restored. To this end a situation is created in which intruders are already in power and are in the course of attempting to acquire not only power but the concrete expression of the ownership, material possessions, and a wife. Legitimacy is set at nought. The ruling family is to be put aside and the legitimate heir removed. The stability of the kingdom depends on the pertinacity of the queen, Penelope. In spite of the activities of the suitors the court continues to be dominated by the myth of the absent Odysseus. This myth is presented to the audience in a series of episodes in which Odysseus approaches numerous homes, cultures, and kingdoms. Although in many instances his actions offer parallels to the intrusions of the epic hero, there is never a question of challenge to take over rule. By far the most important encounters, indeed, are those in which Odysseus has the opportunity to establish himself as a consort to a female ruler or member of a royal family. In other words, he would have become a creature like the suitors, except that there would have been no unwillingness on the part of the lady.

The return of Odysseus to his own palace is described in terms exactly the opposite of those in which the intruder-hero is normally depicted. He lands peacefully—indeed, asleep. He stores his treasure. He is alone and he appears not as a warrior but as a beggar. He reveals himself first to his son. The confrontation with the evil occupiers of the hall comes about as a result of a game and is more like a ritual slaughter than a combat between warriors. The final recognition comes from the guardian of the hall's culture, Penelope. It will be noted that in no other epic do we have a set of circumstances like this. Only in the *Nibelungenlied* is there any question of the winning of a woman, and there the question is distorted by the strange situation of Brunhilde in Island and by the influence of the romance genre. In all other epics the role of women, if it exists at all, is totally subordinated to the conflict between ruler and hero.

We have pointed out that in almost every case, the ruler exhibits profound weaknesses in the exercise of his public functions. In the *Odyssey*, this question is even more complex. The real king, Odysseus, is weak because he has no power. He is cut off by war and fate from his roots. His son Telemachus is a weak ruler, but his lack of power springs from the fact that the bases are lacking. He cannot be a ruler while the question of his father's death is unresolved. The suitors who have usurped power do not exercise it in any true way. Their only concern is to use their dominance for self-indulgence, both individually and in common. The chaotic situation is that which occurs when a ruler fails or dies. Here the chaos is resolved by the intruder's becoming the ruler, not by defeating a king but by revealing himself as the incarnation of his own myth and thus reestablishing the situation which had prevailed before his departure.

It cannot be emphasized too strongly that the *Odyssey* is a work of reconstitution and that the clear definition of what things were like before Odysseus left for Troy is constantly in the mind of the poet. Even the persons who have aged over twenty years are restored to their former strength and beauty. Penelope and Odysseus have suffered but there is no suggestion that their suffering should have made them different or that they should have "developed." Their bed is rooted to the earth itself and is the very image of the permanence which the work seeks to show (xxiii, 190 ff.). The *Odyssey* is the answer to the epic dilemma. The world can and must be restored, and it is long-suffering wisdom, not heroic derring-do, which will provide it.

For here again the *Odyssey* differs from all the other described works. Odysseus is not the great physical hero, the tall, fair-haired warrior who wins because of the strength of his arm and the sound of his battle cry. He is thickset, with dark, curly hair, clever and resourceful, relying on sense more than thews, though perfectly capable of competing with anyone in a physical trial.

He is the man for the rational conduct of affairs, the settling of disputes, and the organization of a peacetime society. Thus his confrontation is not with an established sovereign—he is himself the sovereign—nor with a powerful and self-centered warrior such as Achilles—he had dealt with such in the *Iliad*—but with a group of self-indulgent princelings whose idea of rule is to misuse the goods of their overlord. Yet his victory is as important as any in epic poetry, for it shows that there is a way in which order can be restored and chaos averted. There is a hope that the civilized world may yet live forever in the undisturbed beauty of the garden of Alcinous.

PART TWO

THE CONFLICT AND THE NATURE OF EPIC

We have traced the theme of the hero and the king in the most important Western epics. What conclusions may be drawn about its characteristics and the validity of the claim that it is a determining factor in the structure of the works?

One of the most important features which emerges is that the position of the ruler is rarely, if ever, shown as totally stable. Indeed, it is of the essence of the conflict that there should be a degree of instability. Originally, no doubt, this instability was due to the social forces we have discussed, the collapse of a central ruling power or a widespread movement of populations. The position of Odysseus is due to the effect of the Trojan War and instances are mentioned in *Beowulf* of rulers who fell under such circumstances.

It is more common, however, to find that the ruler is weakened by other causes. In many cases it is a question of innate character. Louis the Pious is a relatively young man who simply has not the personality or force of character to rule. Alfonso is not as weak but he too is easily swayed by one or the other section of his nobles. He influences policy and behavior only through the prestige of his office, not by the way he fills that office. The situation in his kingdom and in the area which impinges on it is such that no very harsh results come from his inactivity. Guntharius in the *Waltharius* is definitely a weak king and, what is worse, a weak king who believes he is strong. All his gestures are those of a ruler eager to show his power and to demand loyalty from his liegeman and respect from strangers. His failure to live up to the image which he himself creates is a highly effective means of showing the vulnerability of kingdoms to the intruder hero.

Nothing could have saved rulers such as these from the results of their inherent weakness but in other epics the instability of the ruler springs from quite different causes. Gunther in the *Nibelungenlied* has not the reputation of a weak ruler. Siegfried is warned of his strength and anger. Yet Gunther proves quite unable to cope with the situations he has to face. Under normal circumstances he might have lived a pleasant if uneventful life and died in honor. Instead he is pushed by people and events he cannot control, and although he fights bravely enough, he dies in disgrace. It falls to his liegeman to avenge him. There is no doubt that here there is implicit weakness in the ruler, but the stress is on the power of the intruders. It is a quite different kind of weakness that we find in the rulers in the other epics. All, and especially Charlemagne, are portrayed as great men, worthy rulers who have in various ways served their people well. Yet at a certain juncture in their career they are unable to make a correct assessment of a situation or to live up to the only true duty of a ruler, the protection of their people.

In several of the epics the age of the ruler is a very important factor. It is most obvious in *Beowulf*, where Hrothgar is described as having been a most successful warrior in his youth and as having gathered about him a group of liegemen of the highest quality. Old age, however, has weakened his resolve, and he is using the fruits of his youthful exploits for that civilized living which is so rudely interrupted by Grendel. He has allowed himself to think that there is no further need for warlike preparations and acts—or for a ruler to sacrifice himself for his people. The result is total control of his civilized world by evil and his total abdication of control. It is clear that he himself would never have been able to restore the situation. His kingdom has reached the stage where the evil intruder can be suppressed only by someone else. Furthermore the poet makes it clear that even this solution is no more than temporary. For decline is not merely a human matter. The old age of Beowulf is clearly contrasted with the happenings at Hrothgar's court. He does cope with evil and, at the cost of his own death, vanquishes that evil. There is no intruder-hero. Unlike Hrothgar, Beowulf does inspire one member of his following to heroic deeds. The nagging question remains however, whether Beowulf was not himself yielding to avarice, the sin of old age, and still more, whether the continuity of his successful rule can be assured. The instability of rule seems to lie in the instability of life itself.

Charlemagne too is an old man. The stress on his age is usually to show his similarity to the patriarchs and to emphasize his wisdom, but pagan voices give a hint of weakness in their insistence on his need for Roland's support. Throughout the work there are hints of weariness, of a desire to take the easier way, to allow by default the success of those who would compromise with the pagans. And certainly at the end of the poem his weariness shows in his tears at the angel's command to continue his mission. It should be emphasized, however, that Charlemagne's weakness is temporary. It stems from tiredness, not from decline. After Roland's death there is the determination and fire of a true king, and the *Chanson de Roland* does not look to a grim future without a true leader. Charlemagne's stumble is a warning of what can happen to the best of rulers.

Old age plays a role in the *Aeneid* but in a different way. Of Priam we hear only in retrospect, but King Latinus and King Evander are very similar to Hrothgar. Both are kindly, respected, and old. They are faced with an intruder whose person appeals to them, who has divine support, but who must inevitably come into conflict with Turnus, who has good reason to think of himself as successor. The effect of the actions of these kings on the story is slight. They can be no more than spectators—but spectators who suffer—and their inability to do more than observe is a comment on the state of their cultures, which are about to be taken over by the Trojan intruders. Here too it is the culture as well as its rulers which are past.

The other sovereign in the *Aeneid* is Dido. No one could call her old or weak. She has performed miracles in her formation of the city of Carthage. Here there is no question of indecision, of failure to live up to the duties required of a sovereign. Vergil stresses the activity, the success of Carthage. Dido's conflict with the intruding hero is entirely sexual, and it is her womanhood which brings about her doom. She dies as a sacrifice to that womanhood. There is no evidence that Carthage died with her. Indeed, Vergil's audience had good reason to know of its power. Here, and here alone, the ruler fails from entirely personal reasons. For a short time she forgets her royal duties in her love for Aeneas. Vergil's purpose is clearly to show what happens if personal, and particularly emotional considerations conflict with the public duties of a ruler. His choice of a woman ruler was a stroke of genius.

It might be asked whether similar criteria might not be applied to Brunhilde. But for her it is the loss of her rule and independence which are at issue. In the *Nibelungenlied* she is never in love with or overtly attached emotionally to anyone, and her ruin is brought about by her shame at the knowledge that she has been duped by a man she had admired and perhaps hoped would win her and that she has been insulted and disparaged by that man's wife. Her action brings about the death of Siegfried and thus the final destruction of the Burgundians but her own tragedy as a queen is played out in Island.

Agamemnon is the one major ruler we have not discussed and he does indeed differ markedly from the great majority. First, he is not a territorial ruler in the terms of the epic but an elected leader of a combined army operating far from its home territories. His position is thus determined by his control over the other rulers who have elected him and by his success in winning the war for which the army has been formed. His election has brought him great power but also very many difficulties. He is not defending Mycenae in any direct sense. The capture of Troy is a matter of honor to the Greeks, but it is not a life-or-death struggle for them as it is for the Trojans.

Agamemnon is thus deprived of many of the loyalties which a territorial ruler could expect and this is a profound source of weakness. Yet his principal weakness lies elsewhere. It is his inability to distinguish between public and private interest. Other kings show this too—Louis the Pious for example—but with them it is incidental. Agamemnon's conduct at the beginning of the *Iliad* is governed by it, and he expresses it in the worst possible place, a council of his fellow rulers. It is the fact that Agamemnon's outburst and Achilles' outraged reply take place in the council that is significant. The measured conduct which is to be expected on such an occasion is replaced by actions which are unkingly on the part of Agamemnon and treasonous on the part of Achilles. It is only with difficulty that actual bloodshed is avoided.

It might be asked at this point what the moral constraints are which influence action. Although, in apologizing for their conduct, both Agamemnon and Achilles say it was the will of Zeus, the actual conduct of the gods on the occasion shows that they do not hold either man to a moral standard. Zeus yields to Thetis' plea to avenge her son by letting the Trojans win, other gods side unashamedly with one party or the other. The deciding factor in the Greek situation is the nature of the kingship itself. It is, as Nestor says, to be respected and cherished—because support of it and respect for it are the only factors which hold off chaos. But in return the king has duties and he must discharge them well or pay the penalty. In some later versions of the Troy story Agamemnon is, in fact, deposed as leader, and the defection of Achilles leads to major dissension in the ranks of the Greeks.[25]

This same sense that only a strong king can prevent chaos is even more marked in the *Odyssey*. Nowhere is any attempt made to show that Odysseus is morally superior. He lies, cheats, steals,

25. In Dares Phrygius (see above, note 5).

and even kills without provocation. He is bent on acquiring and keeping material goods and in later works with a stronger sense of what was morally "proper," his reputation is bad. In the *Odyssey*, however, everything is dominated by his desire to regain his kingdom and bring back order to Ithaca. This is his excuse, and it is clearly the author's intention to show that Odysseus' wisdom consists in the clarity of his insight into what was required and his concentration on achieving it. The very gods in the poem have little function but to help or hinder his progress and of their "laws" one above all matters to Odysseus—the rights of guests. Otherwise he thinks in terms of appeasing them.

The Greek epics have this single-minded concept of the role of a king, but for the writers of later epics the matter was more complicated. Although the pantheon of the *Aeneid* is that of the Homeric epics, the moral climate is very different. Jupiter represents a force for moral order. He has designated Aeneas to be the founder of a city and ultimately of a world order in which certain moral principles are to be exemplified. One of the most important of these is that duty to the state comes before the interests of the individual and that a stoic attitude to personal loss and suffering is required of those who are to lead and form their fellow men. The idea of kingship was anathema to Romans, and it was therefore important for Vergil to transfer the moral imperatives of leadership to all individuals who were chosen to rule. Thus the moral fiber of the individual becomes more important than the sacrosanct nature of kingship, and the best leader is he who best shows the qualities required of a leader. Aeneas, of course, behaves as a leader and is destined to be a king, but his status for most of the *Aeneid* is that of an intruder-hero. What distinguishes him from the characteristic intruder is precisely his sense of moral responsibility, the fact that he behaves as a king-figure—except for the episode with Dido, when his self-abnegation falters.

Such a moral climate made a great appeal to Christian readers of the *Aeneid*. Although its imperatives were not those of Christianity, they were compatible with its concepts of moral duty. The Middle Ages believed that a ruler had duties to religion which went beyond the mere efficient administration of his kingdom. The *Chanson de Roland* is dominated by the fact that Charlemagne is the ruler of *Christianitas* and that his principal duty as king is to the Christian faith and its propagation. There is a higher law than the maintenance of secular rule but, equally, forces that oppose or are destructive of a secular state devoted to Christianity are the enemies of God himself. The true Christian ruler is, therefore, subject to moral forces which are of and dependent on belief in a particular supernatural Being and a creed attached to His worship.

Nevertheless, the fact that an epic was written during the Christian Middle Ages does not prove that kingship will be shown there as closely allied with the Christian faith. Even if we except *Beowulf* as having its roots in a pre-Christian era, and *Waltharius* as being unconcerned with moral values, we must recognize that the *Cid* and the *Nibelungenlied* pay no more than lip service to Christianity. King Alfonso is motivated by pragmatic considerations in all his actions, even when these are expressed in legal terminology. The characters in the *Nibelungenlied* are deliberately shown as having highly diverse moral codes. Rüdeger is a Christian gentleman, to whom a Christian oath has great meaning; Attila is a pagan in whom it is impossible to find a consistent moral code; Siegfried has no set of morals to guide his conduct but he is motivated by certain social conventions, provided that they can be reconciled with his personal cult of greatness. Hagen, and to a much less extent Gunther and his brothers, have a code of behavior, a warrior ethic which demands bravery and loyalty and in particular the support of kingship.

It will be seen that these various codes overlap but do not coincide and it is not therefore surprising that there is little agreement either among the characters of the poem or among its critics about motivation of conduct. In *Beowulf* the general motivating forces are clear, although there may be argument about the degree to which they are affected by Christianity. In the *Nibelungenlied* there is confusion, perhaps deliberately induced by the author, of old and new values and conventions.

In general we may say that a powerful moral or religious code, particularly one which is allegedly prescribed by a supernatural order, is perhaps less important than might be expected. Only in the *Chanson de Roland* is it of primary importance. Social systems and concepts of kingship and the preservation of society are more significant than systems of morality.

We should mention one more characteristic of rulers in the epic—their feeling of their position in time. In some epics, this feeling of being on a rising or falling curve of kingship is dominant. The sovereigns in *Beowulf*, including the hero himself, are very conscious that societies are not static, that there are powerful upward drives under vigorous rulers and declines into tragedy under the weak, inefficient, and old—or overambitious. The concept of time in the *Chanson de Roland* is inevitably Christian. The secular state of Charlemagne points forward to the full realization of *Christianitas*, and its ruler is aware that he stands at a point on this progress. The contrast between the two poems in this regard is very sharp but in poems like the *Cid* the interest is much less. Certainly the ruler is conscious of the change brought about by events about him, but the poem shows little sense of history. The king and his nobles are there. We see them on stage but there is little interest in succession or in the maintenance of the state. The Cid is ambitious for his children but rather as individuals than as perpetuators of a social system. It is not unfair to say that Waltharius and the works of the Guillaume cycle show little interest in any future but that of individuals, and it is perhaps this lack of universality which contributes to the feeling that they are not epics of the highest order.

The *Nibelungenlied,* on the other hand, is intensely concerned with time and rule. The problem here is the clash between the old, heroic values which are to varying degrees present in all the characters and which deeply influence their conduct, and new social concepts, partly Christian, partly the courtly ideals of the romance, which are of more recent invention, which again are present in varying ways in many characters and which clash with the older values. Here there is a feeling of the influence of change, an influence which the author considers dangerous. The *Nibelungenlied* shows society destroyed by the clash, but the destruction is exemplary, not a prediction of the total death of the heroic. Dietrich and Hildebrand, the great representatives of heroic values, survive.

Greek epic too stresses the exemplary. There is constant reference to what is past and what is to come. Ancestry and descent are of great importance, and the actions of individuals are very often set in a frame of reference which compares them with similar actions by their ancestors or by men of an earlier time. Although they cannot hope to equal the exploits of the past, there is an assumption that their descendants will also find it hard to equal their exploits, and there is thus a concentration on the exemplary. The sense of repetition is strong, a sense of cycles of heroes, different but representing the same heroic qualities—the cycle of Heracles and the Argonauts, the men who captured Troy. The *Odyssey* shows this feature perhaps less than does the *Iliad* because of its intense concentration on the rehabilitation of the hero. Although Laertes is still alive, he hardly appears, and little effort is made to show any time-setting for the hero's activities. Greek epic nevertheless is fully aware of the need to preserve through time those qualities of greatness, and particularly of leadership, which allow society to continue.

The *Aeneid* is, of course, set within the same framework and references to great men of the past are at least as numerous as they are in the Greek epics but the sense of time is very different. Aeneas is carefully authenticated in regard to his ancestry—a hero married to a goddess—and the Italian background of Troy is an essential feature of the work. Aeneas stands at a turning point in the divinely ordained rise of Rome. The prelude, the greatness of Troy, ends in flames, but Aeneas brings that civilization, with its household gods and religious customs, back to its homeland in Italy, where the true story of Rome is to be played out.

It is very significant that only in the *Aeneid*, of all the great epics, is there an elaborate look into the future. Both in the *Iliad* and *Odyssey* we are told of the fates which await individuals. When he visits the world of the dead, Odysseus learns what he must do to appease Poseidon and, in very general terms, what his fate will be. There is no long-term view of the fate of Ithaca or even of what will happen to Telemachus. Vergil is concerned to show the connection of Rome with the heroic past and his method is to reveal to Aeneas the glories which await his successors. Time in the *Aeneid* is thus Roman time. Everything is thought of in connection with the city's rise to greatness and although he cannot say it, Vergil thinks in terms of *ab urbe condita*. To him also history is linear but it is the continuing and eternal progress of Rome, not the move to Christian fulfillment. Aeneas begins to be a real ruler when he starts to think forward to Rome rather than back to Troy, when he ceases to be an exile and becomes a founder.

The nature of the ruler in the epic is easier to define than that of the hero. Some features are always present and have indeed been described as "heroic qualities": physical courage which often borders on rashness; great strength which comes close to rendering the person unconquerable; a near-obsession with fame and reputation which is the hero's prime motivation.

It will be observed that these qualities might very well be found in a ruler and often are. The difference lies in the way in which they are used and the situation in which they are applied. In several of the works there is direct physical intrusion by the hero.

The most obvious example of this is in the *Nibelungenlied*, where Siegfried enters the Burgundian court with the fixed intention of winning the king's sister (whom he has never seen) and introduces himself by an insolent demand for Gunther's kingdom.

Here is the quintessence of the intruder-hero, brash, violent, self-centered—and invincible. These qualities are known to his hosts and thus to the poet's audience and it is Siegfried's burden that he must live up to the account given of his exploits by Hagen—the slayer of the Nibelungen and of the dragon. The confrontation does not end in battle, and Siegfried becomes relatively tame in his relations with the Burgundians but his self-centeredness, his eagerness for fame, his physical violence, and particularly his total inability to understand the point of view of others never change. Siegfried has many of these characteristics in the Norse works in which he appears but it is hard to escape the conclusion that the author's desire to contrast courtly and heroic qualities and morality have led him to draw Siegfried in very broad strokes as the archetypal intruder-hero who is the victim of courtly love concepts. The matter is important because, as we have seen, intrusion is of the very essence of the poem, and most of the major characters, including the females, at some time become intruders: Gunther and Hagen in Island, Kriemhilde at Worms, and all the Burgundians at the court of Attila. None behaves like Siegfried, for Gunther and Hagen make a formal challenge but are afraid of the consequences when they see Brunhilde; Kriemhilde challenges Brunhilde with all the insolence shown by Siegfried but with an emphasis on insult rather than physical force. The intrusion of Gunther and Hagen at Attila's court resembles that of Kriemhilde in being the result of an invitation motivated by deception, but Gunther to some degree and Hagen entirely are aware that they are being lured to their doom, and the expedition is an intrusion by a whole royal power into the lands of another. Thus the emphasis in the *Nibelungenlied* is much less on individual intrusions than the theme of intrusion itself, and the author has provided a traditional intruder, Siegfried, with whom the others may be compared.

Achilles and Roland are closest to Siegfried in their personal characteristics. Both are intensely physical, inclined to turn to violent solutions, to confrontation. Both are unquestionably superior in physical strength to those around them and although, in the *Iliad*, Achilles is not technically invulnerable, the thought of his being defeated in fair fight is inconceivable. Roland is never wounded by an enemy. His death is the result of his enormous effort in blowing the oliphant.

A very important characteristic of both is their conviction that their leaders and the forces they command cannot do without them. Their whole attitude is based on a feeling of indispensability, of right to privileges of decision making and the spoils of war. Both make it clear that they regard the war in which they are engaged rather as an opportunity to increase their own reputation then as important in a cause and they resent any action that will deprive them of that opportunity. Achilles and Roland, at the beginning of the epics in which they appear, represent in its most extreme form the egoism which is so frequently a characteristic of the hero, the disruptive presence of a force which is little concerned with the larger issues of public policy.

Their obstinacy leads to tragedy. Achilles does not abandon his attitude that he has been abused and that his importance has not been recognized. His change of heart, such as it is, consists only in the recognition that others have rights too and that harshness must sometimes be modified. Heroism and recognition are still Roland's central thought but he goes much further than Achilles in recognizing that he has brought misery to others by his single-minded attention to his own fame, and he appears to recognize also the higher duty he owes to God and His vicegerent, Charlemagne.

Waltharius is also concerned only with his affairs, but his situation is different. As a hostage he owes little loyalty to Attila, even though the king has been very kind to him, and the attentions he receives from Gunther and Hagen are not due to any insolence or violent intrusion on his part but to the stupidity and cupidity of Gunther. His actions are those of the hero, inasmuch as he enters a ruler's lands and confronts that leader in combat, and he acts only in physical terms with no reference to any higher values than his personal success and return to his homeland, but he has no designs on Gunther's kingdom. We have the curious situation of a hero behaving more reasonably than the ruler into whose lands he intrudes.

The combination of physical prowess with reasonable behavior is also characteristic of the Cid and Beowulf. The Cid's bravery and strength are constantly stressed in the poem. In battles he is the best performer and is deeply respected for his prowess but he does not misuse that power. He rarely boasts and he never mistreats those who do not themselves behave badly. His confrontations with and finally his disgracing of the Carrión family is brought on by its humiliation of his daughters and by their attempts to deprive him of the King's favor. Nevertheless it cannot be denied that the whole action of the epic is brought on by the Cid's upward striving, his desire for rewards and social recognition, and the poem ends when these are accorded to him in full measure. He cannot be blamed for his ambition, but it is a disturbing factor at Alfonso's court and represents a violent change in the established order. His self-restraint is very evident in his relations to the king but there can be no questioning the quality he shares with other heroes, his determination to succeed.

Beowulf also shares this quality. His appearance at Hrothgar's court is an expedition to gain fame. He carefully ensures that the conditions will be such as to raise his fame to its highest point. He is sorry for Hrothgar and respects him but it is fame, not sympathy, which motivates his conduct. His attitude seems to change as the episodes progress. The defeat of Grendel, apparently all that is needed to relieve Hrothgar, is no more than a characteristic "heroic exploit," carried out by sheer courage and strength. The defeat of Grendel's mother is a different matter. The hero must descend to the nether world, outside his own element and do battle with an evil force with a weapon belonging to the creature's own element. The total lack of support by Hrothgar's men makes the enterprise of saving the kingdom very dubious and raises the question, not for the first time, of whether the kingdom is worth saving. It is at this point that the author begins to differentiate Beowulf most sharply from characters such as Siegfried. He refuses to take advantage of the situation in any way. He accepts presents only to give them to Hygelac. His refusal to take over the kingdom on the death of Hygelac again illustrates this abnegation which is so uncharacteristic of the hero. It is difficult to escape the conclusion that the normal self-centered nature of the hero has been modified because the author wishes to prepare the audience for Beowulf the king. It also raises the interesting question of hero becoming king which will be discussed below.

Aeneas shares with Beowulf the characteristic of abnegation but the circumstances differ. Although Aeneas uses war as an instrument of policy, he does not indulge in demonstrations of violence or power. His wanderings across the Mediterranean do not involve him in as many intrusive escapades as those of Odysseus, and the most destructive of those intrusions, that at Carthage, involves no violence whatsoever. There is no evidence at any time of a desire in Aeneas to prove himself, to claim privileges, to insist on his rights, to seize authority—and with very good reason. His movement into Italy has already been justified by prophecies early in the work and the sovereign whose territory he enters is already aware of Aeneas' rights and is prepared to concede them.

Aeneas is thus the only one of the heroes in the epics we are considering who altogether lacks the quality of self-centeredness. He is only too ready to declare that he is an instrument in the hands of Jupiter. Although he carries out precisely the type of confrontations with ruling authorities that are characteristic of the hero and although he brings about as much disturbance and even misery to those authorities as any hero in any epic, his motivation is not self-aggrandizement. Perhaps it is this very lack of ''heroic selfishness'' which has made him less appealing to many modern readers but more easily understood as a hero with Christian qualities. Abnegation in a hero is a contradiction in terms, even in a hero who is to found the Roman empire.

Once again we are left with Odysseus and, as usual, he calls for a reassessment. At first sight it would be hard to think of a character more sharply opposed to Achilles, Roland, Guillaume d'Orange, or even Beowulf than Odysseus. Impetuosity is not one of his characteristics. Over and over again it is stressed that he is wily, cautious, cunning, and wise. Certainly in the *Iliad* he is always on the side of reason and compromise, a man of words and persuasion rather than of violent action.

Yet his career in the *Odyssey* does not always bear out the reputation of the wise and cautious counselor. Many of Odysseus' worst experiences, that with the Cyclops for example, are brought on by the hero's curiosity. In many of his adventures he is the typical brash hero, intent on proving his superiority. He is prepared to push on to challenge the rulers of other lands in the pursuit of purely material gains. At times he appears to be as irresponsible as Siegfried, but the difference lies in the fact that Odysseus never loses sight of his objective—the return home and the restoration of his kingdom.

It is in this respect that he is wise. He calculates the effect of his actions and integrates those actions into his general plan. Thus, at the court of Alcinous he goes through the normal actions of an intruder without any of the violence or bragadoccio which normally accompanies such an intrusion. When he arrives at his own palace he is impersonating a beggar, and his actions, in that guise, are those of an intruder-hero on a grand scale. His challenges to the suitors, when considered in the light of his apparent social position, are extraordinary. He insults princes, he criticizes their bad manners, and ends by insinuating himself into the contest arranged to decide who shall marry Penelope. Yet all these challenges are part of a carefully developed plan, a subterfuge to lure the suitors into committing themselves and ultimately to kill them. Odysseus proves himself to be indeed far-seeing and wise. In him the rashness of the hero consists only in individual actions. In his planning he goes far beyond the hero and becomes the king.

The movement from hero to king is clear in the *Odyssey* but only because Odysseus was a king from the beginning. His behavior as hero is due to the circumstances resulting from the Trojan War, the world turned upside down. Odysseus' change of status is a reversion to the original state of affairs, not a true change. But in many epics there is a true change from hero to king. At Troy, Aeneas had been a high noble but not a warrior of the very first rank. He escapes from Troy, and all Vergil's stress on his destiny and his rescue of his father cannot hide the fact that his wife was left to die and that he did not fight to the end.

For the first six books of the *Aeneid* he is the exile, the landless man who seeks a home. His transition to a ruler, although not to a king, comes about as a result of recognition by Latinus and betrothal to Lavinia. He gains full stature as ruler by defeating the heir-apparent, who represents the forces of the older establishment. It is in the *Aeneid* that we see most clearly the relation between the failing king and the vigorous hero. Latinus has made provision for the succession by an alliance to the most vigorous of the young men about him, Turnus. Aeneas replaces Turnus by divine command and proves his capacity by defeating and killing Turnus in single combat. The situation comes very close to that which often occurs on the replacement of the fertility king—it is the king's daughter who finds a consort. The similarity should not be overstressed.

All the emphasis in the *Aeneid* is on the finding of a worthy replacement for Latinus and the founding of a Roman state. The hero-exile from Troy is integrated into the Latin state but the integration is not bloodless. Although the old kings Latinus and Evander survive, they suffer grievous losses and the old order is shattered.

Whatever one thinks of the structure of *Beowulf*, it is clear that we are presented with a poem about youth and age, about the young and vigorous hero and the aged ruler whose strength is failing but who knows his responsibilities. Beowulf starts as hero and ends as king but by no means in the same way as Aeneas. When he comes to rescue Hrothgar it is to gain fame, and there is evidence in the poem that his reputation was not as great as he could have desired. We have mentioned that a lesser man might have regarded his success as a reason for taking over Hrothgar's kingdom. The thought is certainly not far from Hrothgar's mind

> Nū ic, Bēowulf, þec,
> secg betsta,   mē for sunu wylle
> frēogan on ferhþe;   heald forð tela
> Nīwe sibbe. (946–49)

(Now, Beowulf, best of men, I am determined to take you to my heart as a son. From now on hold fast to our new kinship.)

This offer to make Beowulf his son clearly indicates that he regards Beowulf as the best possible successor to his kingdom. He is right. The destruction of Heorot might have been avoided with Beowulf in power but the nobles around Hrothgar are not pleased. Wealhtheow gives Hrothgar a golden cup but adds the words

> Mē man sægde,   þæt þū ðē for sunu wolde
> hereri[n]c habban.   Heorot is gefælsod,
> bēahsele beorhta;   brūc þenden þū mōte
> manigra mēdo,   ond þīnum māgum læf
> folc ond rīce,   þonne ðū forð scyle,
> metodsceaft seon. (1175–80)

(I have been told that you want to have this hero as your son. Heorot, that bright ring-hall, is cleansed. While you can, make use of these many gifts and leave people and kingdom to your relations when you must leave to look on your fate.)

The appeal is to keep the kingship in the hands of natives, not allow it to pass into the hands of a stranger. Wealhtheow follows up her plea with rich gifts to Beowulf and a request that he support her sons. There is no comment from the hero on this obvious attempt to persuade him not to accept Hrothgar's offer and we hear no more of the matter. Yet clearly the possibility of the hero's reward being the succession is in the minds of all. After the killing of Grendel's mother, Hrothgar is quick to contrast Beowulf with some examples of overbearing behavior.

Neither in the *Cid* nor in the Guillaume epics is there the slightest possibility that the hero will succeed the king. Indeed, the whole point of both is to show the intense loyalty of the hero and his integrity in opposing those who represent the establishment and would use it for their own purposes. Yet both become independent rulers. The Cid acquires a kingdom outside Alfonso's dominions which might easily be a threat to the king if the hero decides to give up his loyalty. It paves the way for the marriage of his daughters to princes. The new kingdom, it may be added, is acquired as the result of actions entirely appropriate to an intruder-hero: he deprives a large number of persons, Christian, Jew, and Moor, of their lands and property. Guillaume d'Orange acquires his fiefs in a similar way. The only land his king will "grant" him lies outside that king's jurisdiction and Guillaume's lands have to be won from their pagan owners. Like the Cid, Guillaume does not try to break away from the suzerainty of his king but he does in fact become an independent ruler. In the hour of his greatest need the king fails to help him and the stress in the poem is less on potential rivalry than on the weakness of Louis and his failure to merit the services of a vassal like Guillaume.

Not the least of the confusions in the *Nibelungenlied* is that all the heroes are rulers and all the rulers heroes at different stages of the poem. Siegfried's brash entry into the court at Worms is not due to any need for land or goods, nor are any of the subsequent intrusions by Gunther, Hagen, or Kriemhilde motivated by a desire for spoil. There is thus no question of a hero becoming a king, except in one sense. To Brunhilde and to her alone of the major characters, Siegfried is not a prince but a liegeman, and it is her confusion about this, brought about by Gunther's deceit and Siegfried's abetting of it, that causes tragedy. For Brunhilde expected Siegfried the prince and is told that he is Siegfried the liegeman. She marries Gunther the prince only to find that Siegfried is her true conqueror—and a prince.

In several major epics the status of the hero never changes. Waltharius is always a ruler. His position as intruder-hero is temporary, the result of accidental circumstances. The most important instances are Achilles and Roland. In both the *Iliad* and the *Chanson de Roland*, the conflict between ruler and hero may be described as internal in the sense that in neither poem is there physical intrusion by the hero into the ruler's domain nor any independent action by the hero away from the power base of the ruler. The challenge consists of questioning the ruler's decisions and indeed his ability to make them. In both epics, although in different ways, the question arises as to who is actually ruling. We have seen that this same problem occurs in the *Cid*, the *Nibelungenlied*, and *Beowulf* but there the hero is opposed to those who usurp power.

In the *Iliad* and the *Chanson de Roland* it is the hero himself who seems about to usurp power. The actions of Achilles effectively deprive Agamemnon of the means of prosecuting the war and his appeal to Zeus through his mother Thetis ensures that the Greeks will be defeated while he stays away from the battle. Roland does not deprive Charlemagne of his ability to wage war, but his actions ensure that it will be waged in a particular way— the right way, from the Christian point of view but not the way in which Charlemagne and the majority of his nobles wished. The pagans think and are encouraged by Ganelon to think, that Charlemagne cannot operate without Roland. This is proved not to be so, and Roland's demise spurs his king to greater effort and recognition of his true duty.

Thus we find both in the *Iliad* and the *Chanson de Roland* the problem of the overmighty subject, the man who regards himself as indispensable and behaves accordingly. Although there is no overt attempt here to take over the monarchy, there is very clear evidence of an intention to determine policy. The result is something very close to private war, the subject of Ganelon's trial and the major theme of the *Chanson de Roland*.

These two epics, in which the confrontation between hero and king is an internal matter, are exceptional to the degree that the ruler and the hero remain in close physical proximity throughout. Roland is separated from Charlemagne as the main body of the

Frankish army moves farther and farther away from the rear guard, but the audience is never allowed to forget that the rear guard is part of that army. In the *Iliad* the separation of Achilles from Agamemnon is entirely psychological. In most of the works discussed there is very extensive physical movement, and the structure of the epic is deeply affected by it. In very general terms, the rulers represent a static center. Hrothgar stays at Heorot, Alfonso at his court in León, the suitors are the temporary and static rulers of Odysseus' palace. Dido is in Carthage, Latinus at Laurentum. Only in the *Nibelungenlied* do rulers move and, as we have said, that is because they take on the role of heroes. Sigmund, whose court is Siegfried's departure point, and Attila, at whose court the poem ends, are static. The result of this is that most epics present a hero who moves often over many lands to concentrate finally on the point at which his confrontation with the ruler occurs.

The most obvious examples of the hero moving in are those in which he appears from overseas. Beowulf does so and so do Gunther, Hagen, and Siegfried when they sail to Island. The effect here is that the rulers' land is being invaded—not necessarily in a hostile sense—by persons distinctly foreign to it, from a different people and different culture. In structural terms a static center is in danger of being taken over or at the least of having its values radically altered.

The movement from overseas is the most effective way of indicating impact from an outside culture but it is by no means the only one. The long and carefully described journey of the Burgundians to Attila's court makes clear the great gulf between the two cultures. In a simpler vein, the entry of Waltharius into Burgundian territory after his long trip from Attila's court is signaled by his giving Danubian fish to a Rhine ferryman. The crossing of bodies of water frequently indicates the entry into a new life, sometimes the taking of an irrevocable decision that will lead to death, as it does when Hagen ferries his man across the river.

This function of bodies of water is even more marked in the *Odyssey* and the *Aeneid*. There the heroes not only appear from overseas when they confront the rulers they must supplant, but have been seriously affected in their actions by the way in which the inhospitable sea has treated them. Odysseus' adventures and the interminable delays he suffers are due to this dividing element and the actual form of his arrival in his homeland is due to it. Otherwise he would presumably have arrived as a king with a number of seasoned warriors. Similarly the way in which Aeneas arrives at Carthage is determined by the storms which have scattered his ships. He comes as a poor exile, not an intruder-warrior. In these two works, the passive divider, the sea, becomes an active element and determines events, and the hero's movements become more than mere transition from one culture to another.

The movements of the Cid present an interesting variation. The hero is, of course, based at the court of Alfonso in León but when the poem opens he has already been driven away from that court by the ruling establishment. His subsequent movements follow a carefully arranged pattern of gradual approach to the court. His actions in exile are far from the court and their "foreign" nature is stressed, but links with Alfonso are maintained first by messengers with gifts, then through personal meetings leading to the marriages with the Carrión princes, and ultimately to the full pomp of the trial by combat. All of the Cid's movements constitute impingement if not intrusion on Alfonso's court, a constant reminder of his growing power—not only to Alfonso but much more to the García establishment. The ultimate challenge is a formal battle with representatives of that establishment and the acceptance of the hero and his family into the highest circles. In this poem the movements of the hero are designed to show an acquisition of power which makes him more than a match for the royal court.

One special feature of the hero's movements should be mentioned, the descent into the underworld. In the *Odyssey* and the *Aeneid* this visit to the world of the dead is explicit and marks an important turning point in the poem. After his conversations, Odysseus knows that, whatever his trials and however impossible it may at times seem, he will return to Ithaca and restore his kingdom. Aeneas sees the future of Rome rather than his own fate but after his return he is no longer a mere exile but in his own mind a ruler. The whole feeling of the poem changes. It is too facile to say that the hero has been reborn, but he does have a different kind of knowledge, which profoundly affects his conduct.

The other epics have no such explicit descent into the lower world but many have some equivalent of the journey. The most obvious example is Beowulf's descent into the mere. His victory in this foreign element and his reemergence against all odds marks him as an exceptional man and proves the strength of the tradition of the death-conquering hero but it cannot be said that Beowulf is a different person on his return or that he sees his way more clearly. He has conquered evil on this occasion, but his way to kingship has little to do with the underworld experience. It is, however, noteworthy that all of Beowulf's opponents in the poem are typical denizens of the underworld, forces of evil who emerge to strike at the world of humans.

In the other epics discussed there is no overt descent into the underworld or any movement into the realm of the dead. Roland, the Cid, and Guillaume certainly descend into a mood of despair but this has no real connection with the realm of the dead. Only in the *Nibelungenlied* is there movement which might reasonably be construed as a visit to an underworld. Brunhilde's realm is remote and fearful but most significant is Siegfried's journey to the land of the Nibelungen, where he acquires his treasure, his sword, and his near-invulnerability. Yet in accordance with the spirit of the poem, these acquisitions do him little good. The sword and the treasure are acquired by Hagen—after he has discovered Siegfried's one vulnerable spot and killed him.

The effect of the hero–king confrontation on the structure of epic has already been indicated. It produces, almost enforces, an "inside-outside" structure, a central passive court surrounded by a moving and not very predictable hero. This structure may be expressed in physical terms, as it is in the *Odyssey*, with a gradual closing of the ring and a final intrusion into the static court, or in *Beowulf*, where the intrusion is early, and more symbolic. It may be a double intrusion, as it is in the *Aeneid*, where the structure is more obviously patterned and where parallelism is clearly sought between the "bad" intrusion into Carthage and the "good" intrusion into Italy. The *Cid* shows an early rejection and then a gradual closing in by the hero on Alfonso's court, the outsider becoming an insider.

In the *Chanson de Roland* and the *Nibelungenlied* the inside-outside relationship is much less physical. The attacks on the king not only by Roland but also by Ganelon and the pagans are carefully organized. Charlemagne sits in council and listens to Blancandrin, to Roland, to Ganelon and many others. Ganelon moves away from the court and returns with peace proposals which are hostile. The structural confrontation is clear enough but it is not the gradual closing in of the *Cid*, the *Aeneid*, or the *Odyssey*. Nor does the *Nibelungenlied* display this pattern but instead shows a series of inside-outside patterns, differing from each other but showing clear parallels, as we have already seen, and culminating in the destruction of the originally "inside" Burgundians at the "outside" court of Attila. There is a constant and deliberate pattern in the *Niebelungenlied* of "outsiders" become "insiders" and vice versa, due to the shift in the determining factors of their behavior.

The *Iliad* shows the least evidence of inside-outside structure. Achilles is never very far, in physical terms, from the Greek army but the poem begins with his withdrawal and it is not unfair to say that the main action of the poem is an attempt to bring him back, emotionally, mentally, and physically into the Greek forces. Again the process is a gradual closing, the defeat of the other Greeks, the attempted peacemaking, the return of the Myrmidons under Patroclus, the new armor, the return and the death of Hector. What may be questioned is whether Achilles, at the beginning or the end of the poem, is truly a part of the Greek host. Like most of the epic heroes, he is a man apart.

What is to be learned from this study of the hero and king theme? There can be no doubt of its universality. Every major epic shows the conflict in some form and in every epic the self-centered hero, eager for fame and often careless of established institutions, is a major figure. Equally, in every epic there is a ruler who, in one way or another, either permanently or temporarily has lost his grip on those he rules and who must be strengthened or replaced.

In many of the epics there is a real question as to whether the hero's success or failure is the principal concern of the author. It is certainly not so in the *Chanson de Roland*, where the ruler remains the central figure and the role of the hero, however interesting it may be, is designed to throw into relief the weakness of Charlemagne and to emphasize the absolute necessity of the subordination of heroic egoism to the good of the empire and Christianity. The other versions of the Roland material make this abundantly clear. A similar argument might be made about the *Aeneid*. The principal interest here is in what Aeneas achieves for the future, not in his personal fate. The tension between interest in his character and sympathy for his sufferings and interest in the success of his enterprise makes the *Aeneid* a human and, in Schiller's terms, a "sentimental" poem.

In the *Nibelungenlied* certainly and in *Beowulf* probably the questions of the nature of kingship and of its rise and fall are of much greater importance than the fate of individuals. The conflicts between Siegfried and the Burgundians, Brunhilde and Siegfried/Gunther, Brunhilde and Kriemhilde, and Kriemhilde and Hagen are to illustrate the necessity for the application of epic, not romance values to the ethos of the court and the ruler. The question of the hero's "success" is never important, whether that hero be Siegfried, Hagen, or Kriemhilde, in comparison with the principles involved.

The same cannot be said of the *Cid*. Alone of the great epics it sets the hero firmly in the center of the stage, from start to finish, and his conflicts with Alfonso and more especially with the family of Count García are to illustrate his rise to power and fame. It is true that there emerges the idea that a ruler must be firm, not allow himself to be run by old and decadent families, and particularly must recognize merit in those who are striving to make their way. In other words, a ruler must recognize the need for healthy change. But the major interest of the poem is in the Cid's achievement, not in the principle. That achievement, however, is in large part a victory over established prejudices.

In both the Greek epics the poem concentrates on the fate of the hero. Homer says that his poem is about the wrath of Achilles—but also about the woe it brought to the Greeks. The reader's attention is rightly caught by the emotional problems of Achilles, Hector, and Priam, but this does not alter the fact that the poem is deeply concerned with the problem of loyalty to sovereignty and especially of the powerful subject and the weak king. The parallel cases of Achilles/Agamemnon and Hector/ Priam mark the two ways in which the relationship can appear, confrontation in anger and loyal submission to duty. In spite of the stirring pictures of individual combats of blood and bravery, the underlying theme is leadership and its ethics. The *Odyssey* does not, of course, take up the problem in the same way. The question is still one of leadership but rather of restoring what has been disrupted than of finding a solution to weak leadership. Homer succeeds in the *Odyssey* in doing something which eludes other epic writers. His hero is in a central position throughout both in physical presence and in occupying the minds and thoughts of other characters but because he embodies the qualities of both hero and king, the poem never loses sight of the central problem, the restoration and then preservation of order.

It may be gathered from this analysis of the major epics that it is misleading to describe them as "heroic poetry," as if their object were no more than to portray the deeds of warriors with characteristics which we have decided are "heroic." The orientation of epics is strongly social. It should not be forgotten that most of them were composed at times and in societies when the distinction between literature, history, philosophy, and didactic composition was blurred or nonexistent and that even when such distinctions were known it was often only to a small literature elite not particularly concerned with vernacular epic.

The epic could not avoid the question of the confrontation between settled ruler and independent hero because the society in which it was composed was more concerned with this problem than with almost any other. We have mentioned the maintenance of order, but there was also the problem of succession. A strong ruler could ensure that a society remained stable and that the members of that society were rewarded for their loyalty by relative security. Charlemagne might falter but he assures his subjects of a stable society oriented to the promotion of Christianity. But what happens when that strong ruler is no longer there? That is the concern of many epics. A ruler may have been good in his youth, like Hrothgar or Latinus, but with old age comes danger. Charlemagne is well aware of the weakness of his son Louis, and we often find that the difficulty is posed by showing a ruler without an obvious male successor. Hrothgar has none, nor does Latinus. We do not hear that Alfonso has a son, although the point is not stressed. Under all these circumstances there is real danger that power will be taken over by an outsider. If the outsider can be controlled, if he can be integrated into the establishment without disrupting it, then the active and potentially destructive hero can be made an instrument for good. This is the solution achieved, although not without fearful consequences, in the *Aeneid*. It might well have been the solution at Heorot, if Hrothgar had had his way. The Oxford version of the *Chanson de Roland* describes Roland as Charlemagne's nephew. Other versions hint broadly that he was the emperor's son by an incestuous relationship. In either case he might well have been the heir instead of the feeble Louis we see in the Guillaume epics.

More often, however, the outlook is gloomier. Will Wiglaf succeed Beowulf and, if he does, will the kingdom survive? We can only guess, but the prospects are dubious. What will happen to the kingdom of the Burgundians? All its royal family has perished and we know of no heir. And Attila's kingdom? It is in a shambles. Attila's son by Kriemhilde is dead and there seems to be no successor. Here it is worth noting that historically the Burgundian kingdom was destroyed, and Attila's power fell apart at his death.

In the *Iliad*, the problem is differently presented, since no one kingdom is involved, but the fate of kings is forecast constantly—the impending destruction of Troy in particular. Again, the *Odyssey* provides what might be called a happy solution. The hero succeeds himself by removing the usurpers. And he has a son to succeed him who has been tried in the contest and not found wanting. The *Odyssey* presents the perfect solution to the problem—a superb ruler come into his own again with a good son to follow. The opposition hero/king is used only to present the struggle for restitution.

In general the epic is pessimistic about succession. Great kings alone can provide stability and they are rare. There are many self-seeking adventurers, but they are not always of the stuff of which kings are made, for kingship involves self-sacrifice, by definition a quality which the hero does not possess. It has long been a commonplace of critics of the Germanic epic in particular that there is a pervading sense of doom, of an inescapable fate and menace of destruction. Perhaps it would be more accurate to put this idea in another form: the only way in which the safety and stability of a society can be secured is by the activity of a ruler who can control it and both demand and secure the respect of his subjects and of those outside his kingdom. He must be able to turn back attacks on his kingdom, and he must never relax his vigilance. Yet the perpetuation of such rule is extremely difficult, and it is the unlikelihood of such perpetuation and the probability of descent into chaos which gives so many epics the feeling of doom. Even when it is absent, as it is in the *Cid* and the *Odyssey*, there is a sense that disaster has been avoided narrowly—and by good fortune.

The epic is as much exemplary as it is entertaining, a fact which the Greeks recognized explicitly and which later imitators such as Vergil and composers in the vernaculars recognized implicitly. It therefore presented the social features which we have discussed and made the conflict between establishment and disrupter, in the form of a conflict between ruler, and often his courtiers, with a vigorous and undisciplined hero the central issue of the work. In doing so the composers were able to deal with a central issue not only of kingship but of life itself: how are we to balance the demands of order and freedom, of law and individuality, of age and youth, of settled convention and the search for a new world?

Life is shown as a flux, a constant struggle, and epic poets developed the convention of expressing that flux by opposing the hero and the king. Odysseus is not the Cid and Beowulf is not Achilles, but each in his own way is following a set path of opposition to forces in and around the ruler which need to be changed and by this opposition the essential structure of epic poetry is determined. What began as a social phenomenon expressed in poetical terms develops into an epic structural element so strong that the genre is inconceivable without it. No epic could be composed unless, in some way, it embodied the confrontation between the hero and the king.

BIBLIOGRAPHICAL NOTE

The secondary literature on the epics discussed in this book is enormous, and I have made no effort to take issue with individual works or viewpoints, since I know of none which has concerned itself explicitly with the theme of the hero and the king as it is presented here. I list below recent bibliographies for all the major works and also a few books and articles of relatively recent date which offer opinions which have some bearing on the theme.

HOMER

David W. Packard. *A Bibliography of Homer Scholarship: Preliminary Edition 1930–1970*. Malibu, Calif.: Undens, 1974.

Charles R. Beyre. *"The Iliad," "The Odyssey," and the Epic Tradition*. Garden City, N.Y.: Doubleday, 1966; bibliography pp. 235–57 in reprint Gloucester, Mass.: Peter Smith, 1972.

VERGIL

Félix Peeters. *A Bibliography of Vergil*. Folcraft, Pa.: Folcraft Press, 1969.

George E. Duckworth. *Recent Work on Vergil: A Bibliographical Survey 1940–1956; A Bibliographical Survey 1957–1963*. Exeter, N.H.: Vergilian Society, 1958 and 1964.

BEOWULF

Stanley B. Greenfield and Fred C. Robinson. *A Complete Bibliography of Publications in Old English Literature to the End of 1972*. Toronto: University of Toronto Press, 1980.

CHANSON DE ROLAND

Joseph J. Duggan. *A Guide to Studies on the "Chanson de Roland."* London: Grant and Cutler, 1976.

CID

A. D. Deyermond. "Tendencies in *Mio Cid* Scholarship 1943–1973." In A. D. Deyermond, ed., *Medieval Hispanic Studies Presented to Rita Hamilton*. London: Tamesis, 1977. Bibliography pp. 42–47.

NIBELUNGENLIED

Willy Krogmann and Ulrich Pretzel. *Bibliographie zum "Nibelungenlied" und zur Klage*. 4th ed. Berlin: Schmidt, 1966.

USEFUL WORKS

Karl-Heinz Bender. *König und Vassall: Untersuchungen zur "Chanson de Guillaume" des XII^{en} Jahrhunderts*. Studia Romanica 13. Heidelberg: Winter, 1967.

Harry Berger, Jr. and H. Marshall Leicester, Jr. "Social Structure as Doom: The Limits of Heroism in *Beowulf*." In Robert B. Burlin and Edward B. Irving, Jr. eds., *Old English Studies in Honour of John C. Pope*. Toronto: University of Toronto Press, 1974.

Mario A. Di Cesare. *The Altar and the City*. New York: Columbia University Press, 1974.

M. I. Finley. *The World of Odysseus*. Rev. ed. New York: Viking, 1965.

Thomas Greene. *The Descent from Heaven: A Study in Epic Continuity*. New Haven: Yale University Press, 1963.

John W. Hunt. *Forms of Glory: Structure and Sense in Vergil's "Aeneid."* Carbondale: University of Southern Illinois Press, 1973.

Stephen G. Nichols, Jr. "The Spirit of Truth: Epic Modes in Medieval Literature." *New Literary History* (1970) 1: 365–86.

Martin P. Nilsson. *A History of Greek Religion.* Translated from Swedish. 2d ed. Oxford: Clarendon, 1949.

Brooks Otis, *Virgil: A Study in Civilized Poetry.* Oxford: Clarendon, 1963.

Denys Page, *The Homeric Odyssey.* Oxford: Clarendon, 1955.

J. Rodriguez-Puertolas. "El Poema de mio Cid: Nueva épica y nueva propaganda." In A. D. Deyermond, ed., *"Mio Cid" Studies.* London: Tamesis, 1977.

R. M. Walker. "The Role of the King and the Poet's Intentions in the Poema de mio Cid." In A. D. Deyermond, ed. *Medieval Hispanic Studies Presented to Rita Hamilton*, pp. 257–66. London: Tamesis, 1977.